INSIDE THE AUCTION GAME

INSIDE THE AUCTION GAME

by

Frank Stefanick

Copyright © 1991, 2000 by Frank Stefanick

ISBN 1-58500-624-6

1stbooks – rev. 6/9/00

DEDICATION

To my wife Dot who has suffered through my many hours at the W/P. Also M. Janusko for the inspiration to continue, and M.K. Rillahan, Town Librarian who scoured the County and State for necessary material.

TABLE OF CONTENTS

INTRODUCTION

This book is for those of you who attend auctions regularly, and truly believe you know how to bid and buy---but really don't. More important, it will provide the basics for the novice beginner so they can participate and begin to PLAY THE GAME.

It will impart the knowledge to strengthen the confidence of those who fear the auction arena as a place to buy. After reading its contents one will realize that skills are learned rather than inherited. Like all forms of learning there is a cost. In the public school, its in the form of taxes. The colleges call it tuition and in the highest form of learning "the self-taught", its called "Hard Knocks". The price of the latter can be costly, aggravating and down right sickening. Much of that can be controlled by reading this book.

Learning "The Auction Game", like any other educational process takes the same ingredients, time, study, discipline, patience, and money. The sequence is only important to those who want to put brains before money.

Learn first, then there will be plenty of time to spend the money under much more enjoyable circumstances. Trust me on this point!

The information in the following pages is not written with an eye or thought cast toward the various prestigious auction galleries. It's not directed toward the black tie set, $2000 silk suits, or to those auctions catered to by stretch limos.

Although some of the same basics apply. The true direction is toward the average country style auction. You know, the one where "the Heart Beat Of America" is the limo. Where jeans and a jacket along with a John Deere cap take the place of the suit and tie! In fact the last suit and tie I saw was on a deceased, who was one heck of an auction buyer. It was the only time I saw him so well dressed.

However, in mentioning those distinguished galleries, I would praise and be complimentary in my comments. There have been times when it was necessary to call upon a really true expert to authenticate an item. I have always found them to be charitable with both their time and information and this would be the place to commend them for their graciousness.

Let us make no mistake. It would be impossible to claim that all situations, personality differences, honest misunderstandings, or those of a fraudulent nature, could be covered in this guide. Rather it could be more honestly said, that it will give you some of the answers and a significantly better insight into the auction process.

It will trace the beginning of auctions in Greece from 500 A.D. to today. It will give others a behind the scenes look as to why auctioneers do some of the things they do. But most important, to others it will be a learning experience of new techniques making them more successful at buying at auction. All in all, it will make you more knowledgeable so when you hear, "*Hey! now Ladies and Gents...what'a ya gonna give? Hula gimme three hundred ta start'em!*, you'll be a better BIDDER and BUYER.

DICTIONARY OF TERMS

It will better serve those who read this book to become familiar with the most widely used terminology in the realm of auctions.

ABSENTEE BID-- A bid left with the auctioneer; in writing or verbally by a person who can not attend the sale. At times this may be done over the phone. One of the auction staff will bid in behalf of the absent bidder.

ANTITRUST LAWS-- The most notable, the Sherman Act passed in 1890, followed by the Clayton Act in 1914, making it illegal to conspire for purposes of restraint or controlling prices.

BACK BIDDER-- At knockdown, the second highest bidder.

BID-- A bona fide offer to buy, made verbally, by physical

motion, or in writing. Keep in mind its legally binding and will be upheld by the courts.

BUYER'S FEE-- A surcharge added to the selling price and paid by the buyer. It's usually a specified percentage. The main purpose is to split the auctioneer's commission rate between seller and the buyer, therefore making it less costly for the seller to sell his items at auction. Let me interject at this point and offer an opinion although I've not used this technique. There may be some justification for this method depending upon what's available for a particular auction.

CANARY-- A trade name applied to auctioneers, in a sense they sing for their supper.

CASHIER-- The person charged with accepting payment for purchases. This person, along with others, are charged with an accounting function and initial registration of buyers.

CLERK-- Records each item as it's sold, along with a brief description. Usually notes any specific condition mentioned by the auctioneer etc., broken, cracked or guaranteed. Also noted is the knockdown price and buyer number. It becomes the official record of the sale.

COLONEL-- Honorary title bestowed on all auctioneers from the Civil War days. I never got too carried away with titles, but I imagine to some it may be important.

CONDITIONS-- A host of various stipulations concerning the auction and how the sale will be handled, etc. Any reputable auction firm will have them posted, in written hand-outs, or announce them verbally prior to the sale. For God's sake, and yours, listen to what's said up front. Whether Suzy's recent baby weighed 7 lbs. or the next door neighbor's wife ran off with a man of the cloth is unimportant---neither is being sold at the auction.

HEAD RING PERSON-- The auction staff individual directing the runners. Depending upon his/her knowledge, they may comment on the article to be auctioned. Once the auction has started this would be the individual to approach with any inquires, special requests, etc.

HIRED BIDDER--A bidder given a sum of money by the auctioneer to spend if necessary to increase the price on specific items while making it appear the items were actually purchased by that individual if the other bidders drop out.

KNOCKDOWN-- The official passage of title of an item to the highest bidder, usually signified by the auctioneer saying "SOLD", or the rap of the gavel.

LETTER OF CREDIT-- Normally on bank stationary, with a current date, stating your full name and address, along with the amount of credit available.

PASSOVER-- A spur of the moment decision by the auctioneer to withdraw an item from the block, "A Take Down". Usually for such reasons as not meeting the reserve price, or no interest at a reasonable starting bid. At other times to jolt a lax group of buyers, or to combat those involved in a "pool" conspiracy.

PHANTOM BIDDER--A bid "picked off the wall, off the ceiling or from the auctioneer's backside" by a less than honest "Canary" to raise the price. Sometimes also called a "Ghost Bidder".

POOL-- An illegal conspiracy between buyers to control the selling price by not bidding against each other. This practice is punishable by fines and/or imprisonment under the Sherman and Clayton Antitrust Laws.

PREVIEW-- Specific designated time for viewing by the public of the items to be auctioned.

RESERVE-- A required minimum amount in order for the item to be sold. Usually advertised as such, or announced at the time its sold.

RUNNER-- Member of the auction staff assigned the duties to move or display the items.

CAVEAT EMPTOR--Although out of alphabetical sequence, I saved this for last. Personally I consider it the most important of all which precedes it. To expand on Webster, it is a purchase of item/s where the buyer knowingly is put at full risk in making the purchase and fully excepts that responsibility at the moment and forever. To a buyer at an auction, let this be the first and foremost Commandment. There is no greater or more important rule.

Like any game, poker, baseball, mumbley peg, or you pick one. This is a cardinal rule of the auction game. If having to accept responsibility for your actions brings great stress to your life...don't play the game. But if you do accept the responsibility of your bidding decisions you'll experience an enjoyment that will last longer than the most intimate pleasures of life.

DON'T DESPAIR DUE TO SOME OF THE DEFINITIONS GIVEN ABOVE, THIS BOOK WILL TELL YOU THE SECRETS TO PROTECT YOURSELF.

BENEFITS OF SHOPPING AT AUCTIONS

Let me emphasize, the reasons given in this chapter are unbiased and no shadow should be cast upon them since they come from a professional auctioneer. For you see, long before I became "The Canary", who sings for his supper. I was a buyer who used auctions to support his family and pay for a college education. Based on that experience I make the following case.

First, let's discuss the common everyday items we use. Starting with the kitchen stove to bed linens. The category of antiques and collectibles will be covered separately later on. Keep in mind when purchasing functional electrical, electronic, or mechanical items during an auction, normally there is no warranty to be passed on to the new owner. The purchaser should be knowledgeable or solicit the advice of someone who is. Otherwise there is a risk involved, just as in betting on the horses or the stock market.

Usually when purchasing items you will be buying at about 25% to 35% of the original retail price. I'm speaking of major household items between one and two years old in good to excellent condition. There may be items which will sell for less, such as dinner flatware, kitchen knives, pots and pans, etc.

Another category which I can think of is power tools. Depending upon brand name and condition, they will be in the 50% to 65% range and at times higher. It seems the men place a higher value on the average table saw than the ladies do on a dishwasher. There must be some good sound reasoning behind that. Probably some female thing the men aren't privy to, or vice versa.

Just think of the money to be saved if one were to furnish the average three room apartment or six room house with just the major items. It would be one third the price. With today's extended lines of credit available to worthy borrowers and considering the potential savings, it's just down right foolish not to buy at auctions. It's the young married's that are missing the "American Dream" through no one else's fault other than their own. A little patience and knowledge of the auction process can bring it all together for them.

I've done auctions of the elderly moving into Senior Citizen Housing which had purchased major appliances or living room sets only eight months before. There have been other sales due to a divorce where the items have been less than a year old. From any of these sales one could have purchased most of the major items needed for the laundry room, kitchen, living room, and at least one bedroom. Many of the items carried brand names such as Lane, Lazy Boy, Kohler, Basset, G.E., Kitchen Aid, etc., and sold for a fraction of the original retail price.

I must admit, to every plus there's a minus.....It would be a miracle that one would be able to find it all at one auction and in the desired color or pattern. But, for the difference in cost, and a lesser finance charge, maybe a little waiting time, plus a compromise or two on the color is well worth it.

One might say at this point, "well if what he says is true, then it may be a great place to buy....but never to sell".

Let me suggest a little project to help you better understand how this all works. If you've bought a new car recently, call the dealer you bought it from explaining that you won't need it any more since you're going to use a bicycle. Then ask him what he will give you for it....even though it's only a couple of months old. I forgot one thing....make sure you're sitting down before you make the call. When you hear a price of between 35% to 40% less than you paid just months before, don't be shocked. After the Rescue Squad has left from treating your near cardiac arrest---just think about it.

It's really very simple....it's used....once it leaves the showroom floor of the auto dealership, furniture or appliance store, it's no longer new. Also remember the dealer has his costs in handling it the second time around. And Lordy, Lordy let's not forget the commission to that person who walks up and says "May I help you?"

About the only thing I can think of where you get an equal amount for anything is if you burn wood for heat. You get warm when you cut it, again when you split it, a third time when you rank it, and finally again when you burn it.

Now let's take a look at the world of antiques. It's no different. If you want to save the profit of the middleman... the antique dealer, go to an auction. Above, he was the car dealer, now he's called the antique dealer. He's the same fellow, the one that's going to gather it all under one roof for you....and there has to be a charge for the roof, floor space, light, heat and his gathering.

It will happen without exception at any antique auction that I will hear the following. Mrs. Jones will say to Mrs. Smith.

"Oh my, look at all the antique dealers here. We won't be able to buy anything here."

From the dealers, I will hear these famous words.

"Well Frank, you've got a nice crowd of retail buyers here. Don't think me and the boys will be able to buy anything, but we'll try'n keep them honest."

Those two statements are as predictable as the rising and setting of the sun. Of the two statements, it's only the latter which has any true validity, but only because the dealers know the true value.

If either Mrs. Jones or Smith or those like them thought about it for a moment, their concern is no concern at all. Even without any inside information of how a dealer operates, they should know in most all cases a dealer wants to at least double, if not triple his purchase price. In most cases he's not there as a collector, but rather as a buyer to resell and make a profit from them or other's when they come to his shop.

There will be exceptions to that rule, and let me point out a couple before we move on. I've seen times when a dealer wished to make a statement to a local crowd of buyers for future auctions. To do so, he would bid most major items to just below their maximum selling price out of his shop or beyond. At the time, he's over paying for a dealer, but at the same time he's investing in the future.

Its nothing more than a power play on his part. He's hoping they may not come to the next antique sale and he'll have less competition. If they do come and see him, he'll have them psychologically beaten before the auction and they'll probably leave before the sale begins. In which case his money was well spent for the future.

Sure, it's a scam. Its simple intimidation, but don't be too harsh in your judgement of him. He just wants to get the items as cheap as he can. Isn't that the same thing most people want? The big difference is, he knows the game and the values. He comes prepared to play every angle he can against those who are inexperienced.

All that needs to be done to combat his game plan is have your own. Know your values and bid him to somewhere near the top end of that value. After that happens a few times don't be surprised if you see him leave. Remember the dealer isn't there for the hot dogs nor the socializing. He's a businessman and his only purpose is business. When it becomes impossible for him to accomplish his goal by his terms he'll go elsewhere and use his time more profitably.

As a mini-example. If you've been to his and several other shops and found a similar pieces priced at three hundred dollars, then you know the first move in the game. In the bidding at the auction take him to $275.00 or $290.00. In fact it would be questionable that one could get him to stay in the bidding beyond $175.00. Heck, is there any difference if you buy it at the auction for near three hundred or buy it from any of the shops that have the piece?

It's really very simple, play his game, but to your benefit. Of course, all of this profound wisdom is based upon the fact you're not living in some fantasy world where you think he's going to let you buy the piece for $150.00 or such.

Another case when pure logic doesn't apply is where two dealers may have had a prior falling out over some other business deal. In this circumstance they will start a bidding type war with each trying to prove to the other who has the greatest buying power.

The last situation is where the dealer has the object already sold for $300.00 dollars. Instead of hoping to buy it at $100 or $150, he may stay in the bidding to $200 or $250, especially if he's already made some below value buys of other items. Then to him it merely is a cost averaging exercise. People have made fortunes doing the same thing in the stock market the largest daily auction in the world.

At this point some readers might come to the conclusion that all dealers are some dishonest lot cast upon the auction scene. Nothing is further from the truth. They like others, are there because some thing or things are there which can be bought and resold at a profit. What gives them the edge is research, true value, and most important...how the game is played.

There is no more formidable weapon you as a retail buyer can have than the knowledge of anything's true value. All one has to do is look in the antique or used items shops to see what the same or similar pieces sell for. You don't have to be a rocket scientist, and if you are it wouldn't help you much....because you're not buying on the moon.

Getting back to the validity of comments passed by the retail buyer and the dealer. When the dealer says, "We'll keep 'em honest," all he's really saying is, "Frank, I'll take it to around 50% or 70% of my retail value. If it goes higher than that, they can have it!"

Prices at auction and why they reach the level they do isn't any mystical formula. As an explanation regarding the examples at the outset of this chapter, let me explain further. Why does the refrigerator which was bought only eight months before at $900.00 ago sell for $300.00? It's really very simple, you're not buying nor paying for any warrantee, no fancy store and all of its staff, delivery and repair personnel, plus all of those fixed overhead costs that any retail store has. And foremost in every buyer's mind is that it's USED. If it stops working after they buy it, it's their's, "for better and or worse". Much like a marriage, one could say. Some would be quick to say, "Yeah, but there's "divorce". Is there anyone out there that wants to tell me about the cost of that little game!

Let me give you an opposite twist in something used with an example of an actual occurrence.

My mother at a young age went with her father to buy an oak icebox in 1914. The selling price was $9.00 and change. She can't remember the change amount, but remembers the nine dollars, because he allowed her to count the nine one dollar bills.

This past summer I sold one during an estate sale for $850.00. One could facetiously argue that in comparison to the almost new refrigerator, they're both used, but those into collecting antiques know the answer is more complex than that. For the purpose of this book that question needs no explanation.

There are always exceptions. Excluded should be those items belonging to some celebrity. Their name alone commands a higher price than normal and that's why you won't see a John Wayne Yard Sale. Think about it along with Elvis, Jackie Kennedy Onassis and all the others who use the auction method. Celebrity or not, when it comes down to the bottom line of the total sold and the cost of doing so...you just can't beat the auction method.

UNDERSTANDING THE AUCTIONEER

Exclude such auctions as tobacco or livestock, where the bidders are all professional buyers. The "canaries" in that arena sing a song in special code recognized among that specialized group of buyers. For example only: since this book is not intended to delve into those specialized areas; the number 33 becomes REENIE-REE, 44 rolls forth as FOLA-FOR, and 55 does a slippery IFTY-I'VE. That's why years ago if you tried to understand the radio commercial for Lucky Strike's, the only recognizable words were SOLD AMERICAN!

It was fashionable for years to be fast in calling numbers, filled with irrelevant filler words, to give a continuous melodious sound to the bidder's ear. It marveled many in the audience even though they didn't really know what the auctioneer was saying. Of course they wouldn't admit they didn't know...that would have been tantamount to ignorance. Then someone decided to find out why so many people at a auction stood with their hands in their pockets and never bid.

It came as a shock to many in the profession that the ears of the novice buyer didn't know what was being said. The most significant revelation was, if people don't understand...they won't participate. Since most who attend an average auction are not professional buyers, and if the name of the game was to get the greatest number of people to participate, the solution was easy....slow it down and be clear in what's said. So today's auctioneer is unlikely to be the speed demon of yesteryear with a lot of extra jargon to create some special sound. He's inclined to make it easier for the average buyer.

Let's begin with the individual that most auction goer's consider the principal party at the gathering, the auctioneer. This is probably the most widely held misconception, for the most part. Although he does play an important role, the true principal parties are Sue, who's looking for a good used sofa and Bill, who needs the radial-arm saw for his shop. The elderly Mrs. Goodrow that just has to have the signed cut glass fruit bowl, and Raymond the antique dealer, and on and on. The bidders and buyers are the true principal parties.

The auctioneer is only a middleman, or the umpire behind the plate. His principal function in the professions usual and customary way, is to confirm that Sue bid $10 dollars, and Bill has offered $12.50, while Mary Jane has made it $15.00, and on and on, he goes. Only the bidders know where it will end......As long as they offer the money the auctioneer will never run out of higher numbers.

As his melodious chant takes center stage, he may break away from calling the numbers. He sees it's time to make a complimentary comment to the lady in the red dress, while coaxing another upward bid. While waiting for the next item, he may tell a funny story, using himself as the brunt of the joke. Or he may explain how the one good shovel and the broken one must be sold together, since they've been together so long it would be a shame to split them up now.

He's there to sell. If the right mood can be created, he will do it in a light and entertaining way. Let there be no doubt that he can not share the stage with the likes of Sinatra, Madonna, Willie Nelson, or Pavoroti, but he knows that to be entertaining... is part of the sell.

This is not to over simplify the good auctioneer as a mere crier of numbers, because he's not. His expertise about the items, ability to organize, professional training, research, and just plain hard work before the show begins makes an entertaining and successful auction.

Although some auctioneers have earned a niche someplace between a horse thief and a less than honest politician, so be it. Buyers who continue to patronize such individuals only continue the ability of such auctioneers to function in a less than honest way. Who would knowingly go to a doctor that has a great bedside manner and cheap fees, but his patients don't live as long as a doctor whose manner is more abrupt and less delusory. I guess it all comes down to value and what is most important...the beside manner and cheap rates or living.

No buyer should expect the auctioneer to be more than he or she is themselves. Don't expect him to walk on water.....unless you can! Take into consideration that he may not be an expert in respect to certain items. He may not know at times that an item is less than perfect, having had only a cursory glimpse of it prior to it being sold. That's the potential buyers duty. If he's an honest auctioneer and knows about a problem, he'll mention it. If not, be fair and shoulder your own responsibility.

If the auctioneer has done some of the work for you,

such as providing a letter of authenticity by a recognized expert, a guarantee verbally or in writing regarding an item, or the mention of a chip, that's a plus for you. But to expect or demand it is foolish and secondly, less than fair. There's an Indian proverb about walking in another's moccasins before passing judgment..... try it some time. If you expect the everyday two hundred piece china set to be checked for nicks or cracks, you check it. You're the buyer and "this ain't some exclusive china shop, lady".

What it may take the retailer days to do in checking items, the auctioneer has four or five hours. And remember what the store-owner get's is new from the factory, what the auctioneers gets is USED. That's not to say it may be in perfect condition, but as a buyer it's your responsibility to find out.

If you should find an auctioneer that is consistently less than honest, simply don't patronize his sales. If you do attend, do it with the knowledge and expertise that will hopefully guard you against a painful experience. I stress the expertise, that's the learning process, and it would behoove you to study well. It is a sincere hope that some of the contents of this book will explain how and where to gain that knowledge.

THE SHADY HUCKSTER

"Hey! have you heard about that bridge that's for sale in Brooklyn?--or--I know a guy that'll get it for you wholesale."

I'll refrain from using a wide brush as I paint this picture. Even in those armed conflicts today which we call wars, reference is given to surgical strikes, rather than wins or losses of armies. So I'll choose a brush of the finest camel's hair to draw the fine line between the honest and dishonest auctioneer.

If there is any one controversial chapter in this book, this is sure to be it. I caution the reader, much the same as a doctor might to a patient about self diagnosis. A particular set of symptoms may not be the result of dishonesty on the part of the auction service. So use a degree of caution before using the following symptoms to arrive at a conclusion.

In a case where the auctioneer is picking fictitious bids out of the air, it shouldn't take you long to catch on if you're in a position to see most of the crowd. Bidding at the average country auction is done in a fairly obvious manner. Whether it be by voice, raising of a hand, or the significant nod of the head, it should be easy to follow.

There will be bidders, who for various reasons wish to remain anonymous which will be harder to spot. But even those can be picked up by the observant eye if you're in the right position.

The fake bidder or "phantom", as he is sometimes called in the trade, is used by dishonest a auctioneer. This is a ghostly image that only he sees. Its the most often used scam in the "huckster's bag of tricks. Another of his shady indiscretions is to have hired bidders. If in the flesh, then he/she has been instructed to bid according to guidance from the auctioneer. This method is used to raise the bid price or in some instances offer protection to the seller in receiving a certain selling price. In the protection situation where the true bidder suddenly drops out and now it has to be sold to the fake bidder, you're apt to hear Honest John say something like.

"I'm sorry sir, I thought you were bidding. That's my mistake, I guess we'll just have to go to the back bidder. Sold to back bidder #33." If the true back-bidder declines, then you'll hear something like.

"Well, ladies and gents, I guess we got'ta sell it again."

Some of these staged happenings can be done in a most theatrical way. To someone who knows how the game is played there can even be some appreciation of the performance.

Chances are that if you stay around long enough after the auction has ended, you'll see that various major items do not get removed. That in itself may not mean anything, since the pick-up arrangements can be days after the sale. But if you see them put on the block at the next auction, it should trigger an alarm.

One of the situations where you are most likely to see these kinds of questionable practices are in an auction where the auctioneer has bought the entire lot that he's selling. It should be self-evident to anyone that the auction service which does business in this fashion and buys the lot...isn't going to lose money. With the cost of purchase, advertising, trucking, labor, plus other overhead expenses, the auction service has two choices. First, buy it at one fourth its true auction value, or devise fancy schemes to insure it will sell at a profit they're satisfied with. Either the seller or the buyer will take the hit, but not the auctioneer. He's in the position to shift that mark where he want's it to be. That's how he plays his game and he's in a position to stack the deck in his favor.

Auction services which work three parts of a business transaction, buyer--owner--and auctioneer, just can't do it with a great deal of honest fairness. I know that statement begs for explanation to both auctioneers and the buying public. Let me do so, then draw your own conclusions.

Beginning on the premise that the auctioneer is supposed to be merely a third party, an agent, in the transfer of property from the present owner to the new owner, when "*He*" becomes the owner the rules are apt to change. Now the buyer is bidding directly against the new owner, the auctioneer. And now Alice's trip through Wonderland begins.

Those auctioneers which purchase estates justify their actions on the basis that some owners have no desire to take the risk of auctions. So playing on that fear they purchase well below a fair price. If questioned at the time about their low offer they sure do spin a story about the right to a profit and their significant risk. Let's take a closer look at the risk factor.

They'll tell the owner about the gamble they're taking by purchasing the lot, but think about it. In the course of conducting his business he's sold so many similar type items it's not the risk plagued by some unknown factor he'd make them believe. He knows within a minimal amount of what it will sell for. In other instances he sells his services as an appraiser knowledgeable about values, but now suddenly all that expertise disappears and he has become an alzheimer case.

Sure there can be risk, but the question is, how much! If he were truly in the "risk game" he'd offer the owner a guarantee of what the auction would gross. If it didn't, he'd make up the balance. When that happens, elephants and alligators will mate and produce offspring.

Keep in mind that once he becomes the owner, you can bet your life he'll guard his investment like a "junkyard dog" using all kinds of tricks to reach whatever goal he thinks is necessary.

Let me give you a real life example and you can do some of the business math.

Two sisters were left an estate by their brother who had been institutionalized many years before. It had been the family homestead. They were good common salt of the earth type people, you know the kind, just plain honest folks. No college degrees and not too many high school diplomas in the bunch or fancy I.R.A's. Just one widowed and the other still married and all on Social Security. The kind of people that politicians speak about falling through the "Safety Net" only around election time.

They invited me to the house for the third time trying to sell me the entire contents. It was filled furniture wise with oak items from about 1895 to 1915. During my previous visits I had explained I had no interest in purchasing any of it and assured them they'd get more in their pockets by consigning it to my auction. By the time of this third visit I had heard through the grapevine that they had received an offer of $1200.00 dollars for the entire lot by another auctioneer.

By this third visit my frustrations had reached a point beyond my control. I informed them about my knowledge of the standing offer they had received and finally blurted out.

"If you truly believe that's the last money in the world, take it. I've told you I'll get you more!" Then I left.

Driving home, I became extremely self-critical of myself. Even though I hadn't taken a complete inventory nor made an exact appraisal, I knew the sale would gross between $15000.00 to $17000.00. In my self-critical state I knew an offer of $800.00 more than the other auctioneer, or two thousand dollars would have bought the estate. Keep these figures in mind, they'll be important a little further on.

The sisters finally decided to consign the estate. The location and weather conditions made an on-site sale impossible so our auction service assumed all the expense of truck rentals, and six people to help move the items to our gallery, all advertising, plus the entire expense of conducting the sale.

The day of the auction both sisters came and sat in the front row, one with her calculator. The auction grossed $15,500.00 and the sisters had ear to ear grins after I reached the first five thousand.

Now the math. Had I purchased the estate at $2000.00, plus my expenses of trucking, advertising, etc. of a thousand dollars or so. My total investment would have been three thousand or a bit more and my profit $12,000.00. Under the same basic circumstances and a commission rate of 25% my gross was $3875.00 minus expenses.

There would be those who would mount a defense and say.

"If the two sisters were satisfied with two thousand it was their decision and I was a fool not to take the situation for what it was." Let me stipulate as clearly as can be...if I'm going to shave the hair of the frog, it won't be from those who need it most.

I guess it all depends how you were raised. We all have our price to cross that fine line between right and wrong. To me, if I'm going to steal damaging my name and reputation it'll be for much more. Try several millions plus the twelve thousand! If others want to sell themselves for a few thousand, I guess that's their "calling", I just don't march to the same drum.

P.T. Barnum said it as best as it could be said. "A sucker is born every minute."

He built a fortune based on that principle. It would be my best advice not to be one of those Barnum characterized.

HOW TO FIND THE BEST AUCTIONS

For those of you who are of a religious persuasion, one can assume that the Lord gave a measure of pre-thought to his seven day grand design and for others who believe it just evolved, we'll take a more scientific look. For the purposes of this book it would be just as fitting to begin the analysis of the auction process at its conception.

This period of creation usually starts for the auction buyer with the receipt of a mailed flyer, newspaper ad, public poster, or word of mouth comment from someone that an auction will be held. There will be those who will receive a personal phone call from the auctioneer well in advance of the sale. This practice is usually limited and reserved to those the auctioneer knows are seeking particular items which are in the sale or those he knows to be serious, no nonsense buyers.

If the notice is in written form, read it carefully. The following definitely will appear, the date, day of the week, month, preview time, and starting time of the sale. Next will be the location and directions of how to get there. Sometimes there will be a special note from the auctioneer with additional information about the sale.

Any buyer should give consideration to the fact that newspapers make mistakes. If something seems amiss, such as if the numerical day doesn't match the stated day of the week, or the travel directions seem vague, call the listed auctioneer for clarification. Many times the scheduling, advertising and conducting the sale are so close, there is no chance to proof-read the ad before it appears in the newspaper. We do a lot of praying that the newspaper get's it right...or that we didn't screw-up in the first place.

The next concern for the buyer should be to read the itemized listing. Some prefer to read the listing first, getting to dates, time, and location later. Whatever your sequential preference may be, it's up to you to read it carefully rather than quickly gloss over it. Read it twice or more if need be, it gives you all the important information for the event. Some people prefer to read the ending of a novel before they begin the first chapter. If that was the sole importance of books and the whole purpose of reading, books should be written solely of endings.

Let's explore a single aspect of advertising a little

further. Keep in mind the listing can't cover each and every item. If a listing makes general statements such as carnival glass, Bavarian china, or depression glass, it can be misleading. I've known auctioneers who had only one average common piece and listed the category giving the impression there was more than one piece. If it were one common piece I wouldn't list it. In my opinion to imply that something is greater than it really is, is being less than honest. I'm sure there are those who would mount an opposite defense, and I guess that's their right.

The cost in advertising space to an auctioneer is at a premium especially where he's paying the shot. But one should look for key words like "large selection or collection of". Not that one special item may not be well worth the time and effort of attending the auction, but an ethical line must be drawn somewhere. If its *special*, then specify its unusual qualities.

The best advice that can be given...is CALL THE AUCTIONEER, his telephone number will appear in the ad. Even if he's not the most knowledgeable person about the item, he can describe more fully what he will be selling. At the time of your call it would be downright foolish of him to lie if its only one item.

Some advertisements are more descriptive than others. It depends upon the auctioneer's budget, or how accurate and knowledgeable he is. Some auctioneers would build a strong defense in that their responsibility ends with "a" listing. From that point on, it's the buyer's duty to come and view the items. This type of general listing is sometimes a ploy used by some auctioneers to get potential buyers there and even if they are disappointed, they may stay and buy something else. After attending several sales done by a particular auctioneer who uses this kind of tactic you'll be able to make this evaluation quickly. If you continue to attend his sales then do it without complaint to anyone and accept life as you've chosen it to be.

Mentioned somewhere, usually near the bottom of the listing, will be "Terms", or type of payment expected. Although cash money is always acceptable, one should not be offended if various types of identification are requested, especially where payment is to be made by personal check. If there are special requirements such as bank letters of credit, Certified or Travelers checks, it will be indicated. If for some reason you feel the request for such information to be an invasion of privacy, solve the problem by paying in cash.

It is wise to indicate at the time you register what your method of payment will be. In preparation for these questions, bring along driver licenses, Social Security card, or other types of I.D. that include a physical description and a current address. This is only one of the ways the auctioneer can protect his client and himself against fraudulent checks, and most should be considerate of his position. If the auctioneer were working as your agent, you would expect him to do the same in your behalf.

Think about it for a moment if it were your items and your things were sold and gone, all you have is checks that bounced. *What happens next?*

I recall an incident where I was hired by an auctioneer to assist in a local sale. It was an average estate, but I guess the heirs in California thought it necessary to hire a fellow from a "Big City". When he required the potential buyers to be finger-printed as they registered, I was embarrassed since they complained to me. I knew many of the buyers. Certainly there could be auctions when this may be the prudent procedure to follow. It seemed to be "Over Kill" in this situation, but to him, it didn't.

Some auction services provide various credit card services for a slight surcharge. If it isn't mentioned in the advertisement, call and ask about the availability of this service.

I've done auctions where buyers have traveled considerable distances, three hundred to twenty-five hundred miles. To the best of my knowledge they have never been disappointed in my advertising, but had I been them, I would have called first.

Last, but not by any means least, this will be the place to take notice of any "Buyer's Premium". It may be called by different names, but this additional fee; usually 5 or 10 percent of your gross purchase can be hefty, depending on the gross of your purchase.

I've heard of some auction services that charge the "buyer's fee" to the retail purchaser while the "dealer" is charged less or nothing. If this is true it would be my opinion that those auction services are pushing the envelope awful close to the legal edge. Race, color, creed, age and sex could be devastating if the right complaint were filed, but that's their problem---if there is one?

I've never known or heard of an auction service that did not advertise it before hand and merely announce it just prior to starting the sale, but then stranger things have happened. If you happen to see an auction in progress and just stop. It would be a word to the wise to ask when you register with the cashier.

DON'T MISS THE PREVIEW

Let me state as emphatically as can be accomplished in print ......this is the most important segment of the auction process. As a potential buyer your time cannot be better spent, whether it be one hour before showtime or three hours the day before. There just isn't any better investment of your time.

This time has been provided especially for you and other potential buyers like you to feel, touch, measure, or do whatever you think is necessary to feel satisfied about the items to be sold. The auction service and the seller have put forth the effort, expense, and time to display for your inspection the articles to be sold. Especially where the preview is the day before the sale, this is your opportunity to inspect, ask questions of the staff, or make notes for research later. If you do not take this opportunity, don't complain later about some purchase you think less than you expected it to be.

Yes, its understandable that there will be times when you just can't make the preview during the scheduled time.

Don't be back-ward, phone the auctioneer and ask if other arrangements can be made. It may be possible, if he knows or believes you to be a serious buyer. At times other arrangements can be made. However, this special privilege should not be abused.

Looking at what should be accomplished during the preview is a major concern, but it goes beyond that. First, a prospective buyer should maintain a certain protocol. The articles still belong to someone else and should be given the same respect and care that you would expect, if they were yours. Remember if you break it... you've bought it at the appraised price set by the auctioneer. There shouldn't be any rummaging through boxes and leaving items spread here and there or all placed in a box which is the only white box.

An incident occurred at a gallery sale of mine that will be etched in a woman's mind until the day she dies. A woman entered just before the auction was scheduled to start. She rushed through the aisles trying to view the many items. Among all the other goodies we were selling that day was a signed Quezal nut bowl. In plain view of myself and others, she knocked it to the cement floor with her huge oversized purse. Needless to say, it became a bowl of many pieces.

After taking her to a secluded area behind the food concession and explaining she'd have to pay for it, that didn't seem much of a problem. When she heard the price of a hundred and fifteen dollars she became ballistic. Being a "yard-saler", to her it was just another piece of fancy glassware. Once proof of its value was established, she paid for it in three installments.

Since neither party, her or the auctioneer, gains any pleasure from this type situation the best policy is to be careful with other peoples items. In this type situation the auctioneer had no choice since he's representing the seller but to charge her accordingly.

Now, after you've been dazzled by all the beautiful antiques, collectibles or interesting practical things displayed, its time you must go to work, and emphasis is place on "*you*".

Usually a preview on the day before the sale will be about three hours. Should the preview be on the day of the sale, then it's usually an hour or maybe a little longer. This is the time for checking condition, authenticity, size, restoration requirements, mechanical operability, full or limited selling warranties. All of this can seem to be a thankless job. However, it will without question pay off in the end. Even if the item gets sold to a higher bidder, at least you were sure of what you didn't buy. Remember it's your responsibility to know "WHAT" you're buying and "WHAT" not to buy. If you feel that you should take someone with you that is more knowledgeable, then do so..... It is your sole responsibility to know what you're buying.

In most cases any auctioneer will indicate if something is less than perfect, assuming he knows, but to rely solely on that source of information is foolhardy. However, if that's your approach and it fails, don't blame anyone but yourself. It's not the auction method, or auctioneer at fault, but rather just little ole' you.

To give you an example how not knowing what you're looking at can become one of those experiences in life you'll never forget, let me relate this one.

Several years ago I had the privilege of being hired to do the auction of a Boys Camp. One of the owners in the distant past was the Olympic swimmer and actor Buster Crabbe. The array of articles was vast ranging from a two hundred foot lookout tower to air compressors for underwater diving tanks. Much of the equipment to operate the camp had been stored in various out-buildings. Many of the items had been gathered to a central spot after a weeks work, while others remained where they were found.

During the auction as I walked with the crowd to the various buildings, two men discussed a residential hot water boiler at the next site. Their discussion concerned buying the boiler for a home they were remodeling. I knew one of the men and just before we reached the site he said.

"Frank, don't forget to keep your eyes on me when that boiler comes up."

When it did, without question he was the proud and happy buyer. Later during the sale he asked to speak to me. He explained it wasn't a boiler but only a water heater for a swimming pool and wouldn't reach a high enough temperature. Realizing the error was his, he asked me to resell the unit even though I suggested he run an ad in the local paper since he paid a hefty price. He refused my suggestion and on the resale he lost fifty dollars. Two years later when he called me to auction his parents estate, we had a good laugh over the incident.

It is self evident to most people that any learning process takes time, self-discipline, money and research.

Mistakes can be both costly and disappointing. If anyone thinks the experts are excused from this human failing, they've missed a whole chapter on life. There isn't any need for a buyer to become an expert in the true sense of the term. But, it's true that the more knowledgeable you are, lessor is the risk of making mistakes. Don't rely on the auctioneer or anyone else. In many cases the auctioneer hopes someone in the audience recognizes the item for what it truly is.

"It looked like a boiler to me, also."

Often at a local coffee shop people will approach me about the value of a certain item and preface their question with something like this.

"I know you know more about this than me. What's its value?"

In most cases their statement is probably true, but I quickly tell them there are many things I know nothing about. Fortunately up to this point in time I haven't run into a Rembrandt or Picasso, but I did come across some type of cast-iron measuring device that was a mystery to me and all who attended the benefit auction I was doing for a cancer patient. It sold, maybe for more than its worth or maybe for less, but it sold.

Trust me on this! The average auctioneer isn't some Greek God like Zeus or Captain Kirk of the Enterprise. Heck, we run across a lots of things we never saw in our lives. We're not anymore or less human than you buyers.

I've always felt that creditability in specific areas is important. That isn't to say a forgery can't slip by, but if you want to know about a furniture item from 1880 to the present, ask me. When it comes to glassware, china, pottery, or jewelry, I'll keep my head above water for a while then I'll look for an expert to stay afloat. Even on appraisals when I'm in over my head on Oriental rugs, I hire an expert in that area.

SHOWTIME: DETAILS THAT WILL MAKE YOU A WINNER

The tent is up, the crowd is gathering, the weatherman has bestowed his best for your corner of the earth, excitement is in the air and impatience begins to build for the auction to start.

First on the agenda should be to register with the cashier, where you'll receive a numbered Bidder Card or in some cases a paddle. This will be the point you'll be asked to produce the identification mentioned earlier. Any and all the purchases you make will be recorded under your number.

You should treat this number as you do your wallet or purse. Don't leave it lying around either during the sale or after. If you should leave before the auction is over, <u>take it with you</u> or if its a paddle return it to the cashier. It could be picked up and used by someone else. All the auctioneer knows is that Number #22 made the purchase and it has to be paid for. Any and all problems end with the clerk's record which is the official record of the sale.

If you wish to have a receipt at the end of the sale, you

should notify the cashier when you register. Some auction services will only make receipts for those who request one, or for dealers since they know it will be needed for business records. In some cases depending on the method a particular auction service uses, if it's not requested at the time you register, it creates a problem at the time the auction is over and everyone is trying to cash out and be on their way.

Now in the computer age some auction services using this new technology immediately records each purchase under the buyer number. If such a system is used then your receipt will be ready just as fast as the printer will operate.

When you have completed registering, take a cursory look at the items of your interest, while keeping an eye open for something new which was not at the preview yesterday if you attended. In many cases it may have been tucked away in the attic or maybe a late decision was made to include it in the sale. If this does happen and you have interest, evaluate it the best you can under the circumstances.

Keep in mind as you socialize during this period or even at the preview the day before, guard against mentioning what you are specifically interested in, or the amount you are willing to pay. One can never tell who is within hearing range. A less than honest auctioneer will use that kind of information to see that the article opens near the amount you've mentioned. Also, there isn't much sense tipping your hand to other possible bidders.

One might also make note of the fact that the opposite of the above is also true. Many times dealers will be critical of certain pieces where they know they will be heard. Most people hearing these kinds of comments will accept them as valid coming from someone who's supposed to know. Little do they know the dealer is trying to convince them not to become a bidder for the item. That's where knowing what you're buying and its value comes into play.

Second, on your agenda is selecting your seat or standing position, if that's your preference. Many times you will hear those who consider themselves experienced auction followers say, "I stand in the back, where I can see everything". That all knowing look that covers their faces has always amused me.

Just stop and think for a moment! Isn't it true that the person supposedly able to see everything is the auctioneer? Well then, wouldn't that be the place to be? The person in the back isn't going to see the fellow in the front row bidding from his lap with the flick of his pipe. Nor will he see many bidders whose bidding techniques are slight in movement. However, as a practical matter, we couldn't all stand next to the auctioneer.

Excluding those situations where all bidders are seated in a very restricted class room type setting, the best position is at either end of the half circle that usually forms in front of the auctioneer. Even in the classroom setting, choose a seat at the extreme front corners. By turning slightly in your seat, your vision will cover about 85% of those seated or standing.

It's from these positions that you can see the same thing the auctioneer sees. These locations will give you the opportunity to see who bids, their facial expressions, or you may see that no one bids, but the auctioneer raises to the next higher amount. In the trade that's called "Pickin' `em off the wall".

Being able to see who bids can be significant, so let's analyze a few situations. If one sees that it's a dealer buying for resale, or John Brooks, whom you know to be tighter with money than bark to a tree, or others would say, "you'd be better off trying to find hair on a frog than waiting for him to spend a dime." In this instance you'll probably be able to out bid them, since neither will be willing to pay full value. Since the dealer is in the resale business he'll only go to 50 or 75 percent of its value and "Tight Wad John" probably won't even do that, but if they were his items he'd place the value near any one of The Seven Wonders Of The World.

Just as some people wear their hearts on their sleeves, some wear their bidding intentions on their faces. If you can read faces like the card playing gambler, it can be helpful in your own bidding strategy. This will be discussed later in the chapter on "Bidding Techniques."

Of course, if you are absolutely sure the auctioneer did not receive a bid, whether to continue participation in this kind of auction is your choice. To continue participating only reinforces his illegal, unfair practice. A greater tendency for this practice to flourish is as mentioned earlier, among those auction services that try to wear two hats, both the owner and the auction agent.

The incentive for those who burn the candle at both ends, gives strong motivation to develop schemes to produce certain results. One of the ways to guard against them is to know the items true value, bid to that point and no further. If it goes higher, let someone else be the new owner or let the owner/auctioneer... keep it. Remaining the owner isn't what he wants to do.

Although one would survive without mention of the following .....go prepared for the weather. Remember the sun won't always shine in your corner of the world, and if it does, there won't always be cool breezes to accompany it. It is better to have the rain gear or warmer coat in the car than at home. Some might think it silly, but a blanket can be very useful in making things com-fortable. If necessary, later it can be used to protect the table purchased from being scratched.

A small satchel will be useful to hold a flashlight, mag-nifying glass, notebook, pen, measuring tape, screwdriver, and pliers. There may be times you will want to remove the legs of a table so it's more stackable in your car trunk or van, or remove the mirror from a chest. In dimly lit buildings, the flashlight is a must, and the magnifying glass is great for the gold karat jewelry mark.

A pickup truck or van is the ideal auction vehicle. Don't forget some rope and a tarp to tie or protect your treasures from the rain. If it must be the family car, then check with the auctioneer before hand about available trucking or temporary storage for large items.

It would be wise to choose clothing that fits the occasion and is comfortable. Although I've seen leather mini-skirts and four inch spikes, I always wondered if those who came to a country auction dressed in such stylish clothes were there to buy or sell? But then, I guess it takes all kinds to make the day.

MONEY SAVING BIDDING TECHNIQUES

In order to explain these techniques, let's establish a list of assumptions. In setting up a hypothetical situation, we must understand that there can be many variable underlying factors which could change the outcome. Some of the factors may be the weather, how well-known and respected the owner was, the accessibility to the location, etc. It's factors such as these that cause identical items to sell for significantly different prices at separate times or at various auctions. But for the purpose of presenting an illustrative case to be considered while having some fun, give some thought to the following.

Initially, let's begin the example with an honest auctioneer without any personal ownership of the articles being sold. Since he will pay all expenses of conducting the sale, one could argue that he does have a vested interest in the items. Also he will allow a bid increment to be increased greater than the already established amount, but will require the next bidder to match that new increment amount. Just as in a poker game, and that's important. The players, in this case the bidders, must ante up equal amounts with the other players to stay in the game. Its the only way in order to be fair to everyone. However some auctioneers could care less about fairness, while other's would argue that all bids have to be accepted. That's the furthest thing from the truth. Think about it? Would you like a baseball umpire to require you or others on your team to hit two home runs to score one run, while the opposition had to only hit one?

This technique will show you how to get your treasures bought as quickly as possible. If you're not going to be successful, you'll find it out in short order, but in many cases you'll buy it for less after you've clearly established your power and desire to own the item.

Now that the stage is set with the bidders who have varied interests in the oak bow-front china cabinet, circa 1910. They all have attended the preview held the day before, except Mr. Morgan. Let's take an imaginary trip into their minds and thoughts.

> Mrs. Dodd is completing a "Turn of the Century" look to her dining area, and the cabinet is the last major item she needs to

complete the project.

At various auctions, she has seen similar ones sell between $400 and $800 dollars. It seems to her the prices just continue upward.

Mrs. Chase is also completing the same decorating style. The foot on this cabinet matches her existing pieces. There were others she saw sold at auctions, ranging between $450 to $750. As her mind struggled with trying to decide what her top figure would be, she decides the final figure will be $700 dollars. After all, the round table with six matching chairs was given to her by her mother-in-law. The sideboard she purchased at yard sale for $75.00 was half of what the elderly woman wanted. She didn't consider that telling the older woman it was only needed for storage in her basement a lie, but just sharp business. A recall of her thoughts also produced the memory of another woman offering a china cabinet to her for $500.

Although she offered $150, explaining she had no use for it. The woman refused. If the old witch had sold it to her, she wouldn't have to be here today, but now she would have another chance.

Raymond, the local antique dealer, had just sold his last

china cabinet yesterday. He bought it from a private home along with other things, and he paid $375 for it. Since his business was built on at least doubling his money, he sold it for $875. This one would fit in just fine, plus it was a fancier piece. He figured his top to buy this one would be $400.

It was his tenth wedding anniversary that brought Mr. Morgan to the auction. Although he knew that antiques kept increasing in value (in fact he hoped some of his stock investments had done as well). Usually he did a great deal of research on his investments, but there wasn't any need for that here. The thoughts of arriving home with the cabinet and the dinner reservations at the little restaurant on the lake rushed through his mind. Feeling quite confident that he would purchase it for $600 dollars, he had borrowed the company truck to take it home.

The competitive battle between the contestants is about to begin as the auction runners carried the china cabinet toward the audience. In the following graph of the bidding patterns, keep in mind the poker game mentioned before and the policy of raising the bid increment. Also one other human desire most of us have, which is to buy for the least we have to pay. After the presenting the excellent qualities of the piece, the auctioneer bellows out.

"Hey! now ladies and gents, hula gimme $950 to start'em?" and down he comes with the count. Bingo! he gets a starting offer at $250 dollars. Calling for the next bid at $300, he automatically sets the bid increments at $50. If for no other reason, it's easy to call and mentally keep track of fifty dollar advances.

After the first round of bidding, it was easy for Mrs. Dodd to know that she could bid higher than Raymond, the antique dealer, since he would be buying for resale. Knowing he would want to double his buying price, that would put his top bid around $400 to $500.

It was at the preview that she first saw Mrs. Chase discussing the high cost of antiques with another woman, and bragging of how she was able to buy the same style sideboard for $75.00. Two thoughts crossed Mrs. Dodds' mind,"I wonder how high is high for her! And surely this woman had looked for the hair on a frog."

Today was the first time she had seen the other bidder, but she heard him addressed as Mr. Morgan. The clothing he wore, plus an air of confidence, seemed to indicate that he could well afford to pay top dollar or beyond. It was he who concerned Mrs. Dodd most.

At the start of the second round of bidding, Mrs. Dodd raises the bid increment from $50 to $100. With this move, she eliminates Raymond the antique dealer from the game. Mrs. Chase's follow-through puts the price at $600 and $700 to the next bidder. Since Mr. Morgan was sure $600 was the highest value of the piece, and without any research, he misses his golden opportunity. Which will be explained later when we evaluate each bidders strategy.

Mrs. Dodd makes her second power move and increases the bid again, increasing the bid increment to $200, raising the price to $800. The next bidder would be required to take it to least a $1000 which would have been well over its value. As the auctioneer calls for a thousand dollars, no further offers are made, he cries out sold to "Number #33 for $800".

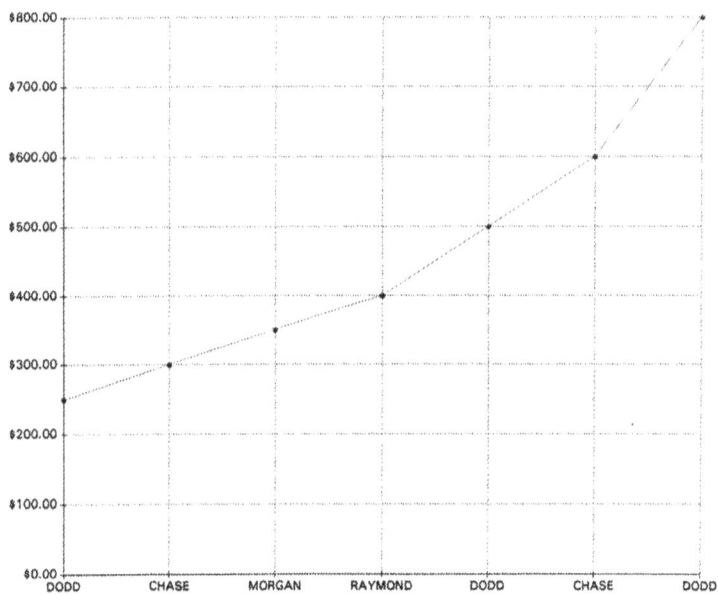

Who were the losers? Well if Raymond, the dealer, had been satisfied with a profit of a hundred or so, he could have used the same technique. Buying at an auction isn't the same as from a private home where the dealer may be the only one making an offer. In many home situations the seller doesn't know the true value of what he's selling and the dealer's not about to tell him. That gives Raymond an opportunity for much more profit.

If Mr. Morgan had done as much research on the value of the cabinet as he does on his stock investments, he could have accomplished the same thing as Mrs. Dodd. Mr.

Morgan could have been the next bidder after Mrs. Chase at $600 and raised the bid increment just as Mrs. Dodd did to $800.

Knowing what we know about the bidders, he would have been the buyer at a fair price, and made the dinner at the restaurant more enjoyable.

Then there is Mrs. Chase and all those like her, who feel that everything has to be a steal. It could be assumed, I guess, that eventually someone will let her do that very thing. Or she will convince someone she just needs the cabinet for canned goods storage in her basement and buy one for $75.00 like she did with the sideboard, but not here, cause its an auction and others are as interested as she in the piece. What's important is knowing the item's value.

Since there are pros and cons about everything, this bidding technique should not be excluded from that consideration. A buyer should remember that it is the sole option of the auctioneer to allow such bidding policies as requiring every increase to be the same amount. It should be discussed by you as a buyer beforehand, by asking the auctioneer how he handles such situations.

There are those of my colleagues who would argue strongly against this type of bidding practice, saying a bid is a bid, and all bids should be accepted. It would seem less than reasonable for the auctioneer to accept a dollar bid when everyone else is bidding twenty-five. On the other hand for him to allow the increase to be so large as to cause the items to sell consistently below their reasonable value would be just as foolish. It may be at such a time that you may witness the *Moses Syndrome* kick in and the auctioneer will slit the baby in half. He will announce that the bid increment can only be increased by a limited amount.

Keep in mind, he wants you to bid more than it's worth, but not less, since he's judged by the owner on the more than, not some lesser value. I realize that may be difficult for some reader's to grasp, but all one has to do is put themselves in both positions---the buyer and seller--at the same time. When you're the buyer---keep it low, when you're the seller---take it to the moon. If you're the auctioneer you hope everything heads through the roof for the moon. Oh God, I wish the auctioneer's prayers where answered!

In most cases requiring a increased bid to be matched means the item will reach a reasonable top figure sooner, while producing more dollar sales per hour for the auctioneer, a quicker buy for the highest bidder and a faster paced auction for all bidders. It give respect to the those who recognize the true value of the item and are willing to pay and move on. It treats all bidders equally, by requiring them all to ante up the same amount of money for at least one sequential round of bidding. There is also the possibility that after that round is completed, the bid increment might be reduced, or "cut" as it's called in the trade. Also keep in mind that the faster things move along, the quicker the items of particular interest to you or other people come to the block.

A brief discussion of the "cut bid" is pertinent at this time in order to understand how it can be used in one's bidding strategy.

At this point let's talk about a "cut bid". Of course the most obvious reason for "cutting" the bid increment would be that a bidder feels the amount is reaching his limit too quickly. This technique is mostly used by dealers. They recognize a momentum has developed among the other bidders and they're going to bid without thinking. The increments are large enough that one bid will suddenly put the item beyond their reach.

Usually the request for the change is made by holding

one finger pointed upward with one from the other hand held mid-way to the upright one. Another signal is a sideways slashing movement of the hand. The ones which always bring fire to my eyes are the cuts producing $1.50 or $13.50 dollar increment. Try counting quickly using these dollar increments up to a hundred.

To use the "cut bid" to your benefit try this. It worked well for me back in the fifties while I was working my way through college. Let's suppose I had decided a particular piece was worth $40.00 tops and the first bid was at $2.00, with $2.00 dollar increments. I would actively bid along with the others while my body language and facial expressions would clearly indicate my dissatisfaction and disbelief that such a piece was worth the money being bid. Remember I'm willing to pay $40.00.

When it reached $18.00, I'd cut the bid in half. That would send a message to the other bidders I was ready to fold and give up. It would also send another message, now that the bid was reduced chances were that the piece might sell for less. I'd let it be taken at a dollar a clip to $20.00, then in as loud a voice as I could muster I'd raise it to $25.00.

Let's assume the auctioneer did not require the

following bidder to match my increase. Chances are the shock of the four dollar increase would delete some bidders, and the remainder would continue to bid. My next move would come at $30.00 dollars and I would raise it to a $7.50 increment. At this point either I'll blow them all away and buy the piece for less than $40.00 or someone else would be its owner at whatever the auctioneer was going to accept. Once I took it close to my $40.00 dollar limit it had no further value to me.

"Let's get it done and move on to the next item!"

If I'm there as a serious buyer, I want to get my business done and be off to sell and profit from what I've bought. If not that, then at least I want to get home with my new treasure and enjoy looking at it with a cold beer in my hand.

There is another form of bidding when it is impossible to attend a particular auction. Reasons can vary from previous commitments to long out of state travel distances. It only takes a phone call to the auction service authorizing them to bid in your behalf as an absentee bidder. They may require you to fill out a special form, or make a deposit of a percentage of the bid, which is refundable if you are not the buyer. If you're a regular local buyer, it's merely a phone call.

In the event you intend to use the absentee bid, or as some call it, the left bid system, there are some things you should clarify. First, does this auctioneer allow the bid to start from the floor, or does he start the bid at whatever amount you may leave? Some auctioneers will open the bid with your absentee offer, or at some percentage less than the amount you have specified, assuming he has not received another bid.

Of all the procedures mentioned, the most fair one is to let the attending crowd start the bidding. There could be exceptions to this procedure, but they should be rare. All your absentee bid should mean is that you will pay up to a maximum amount. However, should it not reach that maximum amount, then you should be able to buy it for less. It should be handled just as if you were in the front row doing your own bidding. For example, don't just offer $100.00 under that kind of arrangement, and if you were there, you'd hear something like this.

"Hey! now Ladies and Gents, we got'ta a hundred dollar starting bid on this, hula gimme one twenty-five."

There are two ways to leave this kind of bid, either up

to a specific amount, or up to an amount plus one increment. Let's take a look at both approaches.

In leaving an absentee bid of up to a specific amount, you tie the auctioneer's hands when certain sequences take place which he has no control over. For example, let's suppose a bid was left for $100. The bid developed from the floor, starting at $80. The increments were $5.00, so a member of the auctioneer's staff bids the absentee bidder in at $85, then again at $95. The bidder from the floor bids $100, and without any other bid, buys the article. As you can see, the auction staff could only take the absentee bidder to $95 dollars because of the amount it started at and the following sequence.

Now taking the same example, let's take the absentee bid of up to $100, plus one increment. The bid from the floor starts at $80 and the member of the auction staff puts the absentee bidder in at $85, $95, and $105, which in many cases will buy the article.

A legitimate question would be,"Yes, but how do I know where it's going to start, what will the increment be and a just concern that you don't pay more than you should, or more than you can afford?" Just as legitimate, the answer could be, there is no completely positive way to know. But you can usually come very close if you know the true value of the item and the auctioneer is an honest one.

If you know the auctioneer to be honest, his conduct will mirror that quality and tell him so. After all it would be foolish of him to tell you that it sold for a hundred when it only sold for eighty-five, not being aware of who was in the crowd that would mention it to you. Next, how do you figure the increment amount? Usually the importance and value of the article will indicate the increment amount. That's where your research and knowledge of antique shop prices or the many published books giving such information can be of help.

Since the overall value of the item enters into the increment decision. A good guess would be that for something worth a hundred dollars, it would be a $5, $10, or maybe a $12.50 increment. Anything is possible, but it would be rare to be greater. Up to two hundred, you're probably safe up to $25.00. At three hundred to a thousand, probably $50 to $100 would be as good a guess as any. Usually as the estimated value of the item gets greater, so goes the increments amounts. It would be a stretch of the imagination for the Mona Lisa to be taking a hundred dollar increment shot.

Yes, strange things happen at auctions, but if its going to be that unusual, somebody let me know, I'd sure like to be there to witness the event.

Now how does one match this all together with the value. Let's restrict value to mean, what you're willing to pay for the article. I know that may seem a difficult question at times, but it's one that must be made.

For the purpose of this book I'll not delve into the psychological avenues that people may use to reach that conclusion. That would be a topic for another book and impossible to devote enough time to it now, nor the research from my minor in Psych #101 necessary to do it justice at this point for the reading audience.

Whatever the considerations, you've got to be the one who makes them. There are two roads one might take to arrive at the same destination. First, what's the maximum you want to pay for the item. We can assume any lesser amount you can live with any time. I prefer the higher road. If I feel it's a hundred dollar article, I could live with another $5, $10, or maybe $25 more, assuming it's for my home. So I might place the bid at $100 plus one increment. The second alternative would be to tell the auctioneer he has a "Starting Bid" of $125. Then I would hope and pray that my bid was so overwhelming no one would bid $126.00. As one can see there are different roads to take. You can choose that which is most comfortable for you.

In the actual auction setting, the auctioneer will usually announce an absentee bid and indicate which of his staff will do the bidding in behalf of the person not in attendance. When the bidding is finished, the auctioneer may allow only the back bidder or any attending bidder to see the absentee bid.

This is his sole option. I have always made that option known before the bidding starts. I have always felt its only fair that after the bidding is finished, the name, address, and phone number of the absentee bidder should be available to either the successful bidder or back-bidder present, but no one else.

Let me make mention of bidding by phone which is another form of absentee bidding. Although it would be rare at a country estate auction due to limited phone facilities. It could the wave of the future with cellular phones becoming more popular.

Possibly this is a good spot for some personal reflective thoughts of mine regarding all forms of absentee bidding. Like many accepted things of the modern world there are some things I don't feel comfortable with. Absentee phone bids is one of them. I've handled written ones and will continue to do so, but I see phone bidding by its nature alone, fraught with potential dishonesty.

Who knows who's on the phone or that anyone is on the other end of the line? I suppose speaker phones that would convey the conversation to those in attendance may eliminate the problem, but those situations which I have observed did not. The use of telephones produces additional discomfort in maintaining the kind of creditability with the audience that I felt most difficultly with.

Again, there just isn't a more important thing that can be said to guide you through what might be those uncharted perilous waters. First, know the value of your interest. Second, arrive at what you consider your top price. If it goes beyond that, LET SOMEONE ELSE OWN IT.

Many in the auction profession have constantly fought to over-throw the shadow of dishonesty cast upon it for various reasons and some of its own making. I question whether the efforts of the honest professionals are as dramatic or decisive as throwing the money lenders from the temple, but such as those efforts maybe, organizations such as the National or various State Auctioneers Associations should make a stronger effort in this regard. Many of their eloquent and profoundly stated measures fall far short of policing illegal or improper practices. One might conclude that the membership registration fee they receive is more important.

Since no auctioneers which I know can accomplish any of the other miracles of the man who walked in sandals and flowing robes, that brings to mind the most egregious act of all, pool bidding.

Although this is a type of non-bidding, the pool-bid is probably best covered in this section. It occurs mostly among dealers, but could involve auctioneers who use paid or phantom bidders to artificially increase or decrease the price of items they own or they wish to buy.

A reader might justifiably ask?

"Why or how could they want to do both, increase or decrease. Let's first handle the "decrease".

In 1890 the Federal Government saw fit to pass the Sherman Antitrust Act with additional legislation in 1914 and 1917. These laws made it illegal for parties to conspire for the purpose of controlling prices of goods or services.

Those found guilty of these practices can receive fines and/or imprisonment.

The conspiracy in the auction setting operates in the following manner. In the pool, dealers agree not to bid against each other on items of their interest. Only one of them will bid on the item, therefore depressing the price. Once the piece is purchased, the pool members will hold their own private auction. Any additional money that each piece brings in this auction is divided among the members. In other cases a flat fee is paid to the other members of the pool for not bidding.

These practices have not only touched the backwoods country auctions, but also some of the most prestigious galleries. However, in January 1987, the U.S. Justice Department filed charges under the Sherman Antitrust Act against four southeastern Pennsylvania and southern New Jersey dealers. The maximum penalties for these practices is a three year prison term, along with a fine of $250,000.00

More recently in August 1991, as reported in a leading New York city paper, a dealer from N.Y.C., and another in Danbury, Conn., pleaded guilty to conspiracy under the Antitrust laws. They were dealers in high quality early

American furniture. The fines levied were $100,000 and $50,000 respectively.

In the plea agreements, both groups have agreed to assist in on going investigations. It wouldn't be difficult to understand why. If a lesser prison term or a reduced fine is in order, the party under investigation could become very cooperative in order to save his own skin. Any dealer who involves himself in a pool with the idea that another would never inform on other members must be out of touch with the real world.

To further exemplify the rationalization and acceptance of this illegal act, let me quote from a conversation with a well established female antique dealer. She was both a seller and buyer at my auctions.

During a visit to my home with her husband, the subject of pool bidding came up. She listened patiently as I explained my position against such practices not only as an auctioneer, but many years previous as a buyer. Then she answered in a voice filled with chagrin toward what she considered my lack of understanding.

"But Frank, every dealer does it."

It might be old fashioned or to use a modern term, politically incorrect, but when I have to live my life according to the accepted illegal doctrine of others...I'll do something else. As a footnote, that particular dealer and I no longer do business together.

Even more ironic is the matter of the dealer who sells at auction and wants to increase the bid by bidding themselves. If there was ever a "wolf in sheep's clothing...this is it bigtime." Even historical fact is more honest in clearly stating Karl Marx's wife prostituted herself so he could write his Manifesto. Not all, but many dealer's don't care what is takes to make a profit. The majority of this category of people still maintain they practice normal good business. I guess that's why we have a President who redefines what "is" is.

Who's going to be the first bidder? Like in any profession there are those "old wives tales" or "tricks of the trade" whose roots seem to stem from the beginning of time. To be or not to be the first bidder is one of them.

There will be those who would argue vehemently, not to be the first bidder. If waiting for the auctioneer to come down and down has some effect on the final selling price, I've failed to see it. It may be true on some lesser quality items. But, in general the price will rise to some higher level dependent upon its rarity, quality, and desirability among the bidders. In short, it's not where it starts that's important, but rather where it winds up. That is a truism beyond refute.

In conclusion of this chapter on bidding let me cover some general comments. They may seem unrelated, but since the core of the auction process is based upon an offer and following counter offers, they are the smaller gears which make the whole become a reality in their turning.

Taking into consideration that under the Uniform Commercial Code and the laws governing auctions, it's presumed that all items offered for sale are done so with a reserve. A "reserve being the least amount the owner will accept. With that presumption in mind, it becomes a mere refusal to sell by the auctioneer in consideration of some protection to the owner. The belief that an item must be sold once it's offered is like believing the stork delivers babies. Those unfamiliar with the law still believe the requirement to sell is a must regardless of price. It just isn't so.

The exception to the implied reserve is where specific notice is given to the contrary such as,"Absolute", "Sold Without Reserve", or "To Be Sold Regardless Of Price". In this day and age, most reputable auctioneers would pass over a major item before they allowed it to be sold for a ridiculous price.

Keep in mind to truly feel the pulse of this book one must view many of its statements both from the seller's perspective, the agent auctioneers and at the same time the buyers.

"Do unto others as you would have them do unto you."

Many has been the time when I've had the opportunity to chide the crowd saying.

"Gee, if we would have started where I first asked, we'd been finished with this piece and had two others sold."

Some will laugh, and others will suffer some embarrassment, dropping their eyes to the floor. And last but not least, there will be a scowl or two from the ones who offered the low starting bid. The display of contempt is because they didn't buy it or because they had to pay more than the first bid.

Initially, it seems their displeasure is directed specifically towards the auctioneer. Maybe that's because they dislike hearing the truth. In reality, the auctioneer had little to do with the cause of their agitation. It was the others who wanted to pay more. All the auctioneer did was call out the higher bids as they were offered.

It was Ben Franklin who said, "Waste neither time nor money, but make the best use of both."

That proved for me to be the best approach. During my college years and when both buying and selling were important to me. The name of the game was "let's get it sold. Where it starts doesn't mean a damn thing, but where it finishes, DOES!"

Although we know someone has to be first, if the wait and see philosophy adds to some buyer's enjoyment.....so be it. On the other hand in some cases if the auctioneer passes over the item, and refuses to bring it back to the block, its history!

Its time to break-away from all the tech stuff and tell a little relevant story regarding this kind of situation.

Last fall I sold the contents of a small estate in a small iron mine community. The mine had been closed some twenty years and now its only claim to notoriety was that it hosted a prison which contained those that society doesn't want walking the streets. Initially I said to myself, "How will I ever get anyone to come to this out of the way place?" But they came...by the droves.

On my initial walk-through there was a base cabinet in the basement that caught my eye. To you antiquer's, I thought it to be the bottom part of a baker's cupboard; to the rest of you, the home made fore-runner to the now much sought after Hoosier Cupboard. After further inspection, that wasn't the case, but it was still a great cabinet with a lot of practical potential.

Its zinc top was paint splattered, drawers filled with parts to who knows what and the bottom doors, with larger unrecognizable items. You know, the kind of collection that if assembled would have put the astronaut on the moon for half the price.

"And ladies and gents what'a ya gonna give? Hula gimme a hundred to start'em?....Well then seventy-five....a fifty dollar bill...Let's get'em started at twenty-five!

Up to that point it was a wild auction, but now...nothing ...nada. Up to this point the crowd snapped up plywood boxes nailed together from jewelry case to foot locker size at $75 to $125.

Having come down to $25 with no takers, I yelled to the clerk, "Put it on my bill." It is rare for me to buy at my own auction since I've always felt my sales are for the one's who come, not me. If I want to buy I'll go to another auctioneers auction and be just another buyer in the crowd.

I really didn't want the cabinet, but I did it to shock the crowd into realizing I was there to sell and get the job done I was hired to do.

After the sale was over and I had answered natures call after seven hours of calling numbers, two women approached me asking that the cabinet be put up again. By then much of the crowd was gone and the remainder were carrying off the items they'd bought earlier.Since the one woman had done this before I answered "no". I put in a following auction and it sold for $350.

"What's wrong with this picture?" Its simple, just be as fair as you would want others to be if it were yours. Is it too much to expect under the circumstances at a given point in time for a third party; an auctioneer; between the seller and the buyer to ask for something more than $25 for something worth more.

In those cases where the auctioneer does agree to return the item to the block in most cases, he will dictate what the starting bid will be. Remember he's there to do business by representing the owner and certainly to profit from his effort, but not to play childish games.

TIPS ON AUCTION RULES FROM A PROFESSIONAL

The reputable auction service will not be elusive about how they intend to conduct their sale. Usually the rules will be posted in a conspicuous place or be part of the Bidder Card you receive. Although the rules may differ from service to service, the sample shown is one of the types. If there isn't any rules...beware.

It would be wise for those considering purchasing rare expensive items, real estate, or registered livestock, to obtain additional information regarding rules or terms. Usually an attorney can be of some assistance rather than just signing some "ON The Spot Contract". In some cases involving very expensive items, the auction service will require the participating bidder on a particular expensive item to acknowledge each of their bids by signature. This procedure is a safeguard against a bidder having second thoughts about the purchase later and all the problems that kind of situation creates.

If the service is from out of state it would be beneficial

to know if they are bonded in the state where the auction is taking place. The insurance bond can save a buyer considerable money if a dispute arises between buyer and auctioneer. In such a case the insurance bond will pay off assuming the claim is legitimate. It can be expensive to pursue such problems across state lines.

Sample Form

CONDITIONS OF SALES

The property in today's auction will be offered by the Auctioneer as agent for the Consignor, according to the following terms and condidions. Any additional terms or condidions shall be announced by the Auctioneer at the beginning of the auction.

1. All property is sold "as is," and ALL SALES ARE FINAL. Property is open to thorough public inspection, and it is the bidder's responsibility to determine condidion, etc.
2. Though all description and commentary are believed to be correct, neither Auctioneer nor Consignor makes any warranties of representation of any kind with respect to property, and in no event shall be held respinsible for having made or implied any warranty of description, genuineness, authorship, attribution, provenance, period, culture, source, origin, condition, etc.
3. A bid by any person shall be conclusive proof that the person has made themselves acquainted

with these conditions of sale and has agreed to be bound by them.

4. The buyer shall be the highest bidder unless the Auctioneer determines that the opening bid is not commensurate with the value of the article from the sale; and if, having acknowledged an opening bid, he decides that any advance thereafter is not of sufficient amount, he may reject the advance.

5. Should a tie or dispute arise between two bidders, the auctioneer shall, at his sole discretion, (a) determine the successful bidder, or (b) reopen the bidding between the highest bidders until the article is sold. If any dispute arises after the auction, the Auction Sale Record shall be conclusive in all respects.

6. Upon the fall of the Auctioneer's hammer and/or when the Auctioneer says "sold," title to the offered lot or article will pass to the highest bidder who, thereupon (a) assumes full risk and responsibility therfore, and (b) shall pay the full purchase price therefore, or such part as the Auctioneer may require.

7. The Auctioneer may have available carriers or packers as a convenience to buyers, but assumes no responsibility for their actions. Purchased items must be removed after the auction, unless other specific arrangements have been made with the Auctioneer.

8. The Auctioneer may, as a courtesy, undertake to make "left bids" for responisible parties in their absence, under the procedures set forth by the Auctioneer.

9. The Auctioneer reserves the right to withdraw any item before or during the auction.

10. Prior to removal of purchases, payment must by made in cash, or by other means as announced by the Auctioneer. Unless exempted by law, the purchaser shall pay any and all applicable taxes.

11. Neither the Auction Service, Property Owner nor the Consignor shall be liable for any personal injury on the premises where the auction shall be held.

12. Unless the auction is advertised and announced as a sale without reserves, the vast majority of items offered for sale are sold regardless of price and without minimum bid. On occasion, in order to offer the widest selection of merchandise possible, which would otherwise be unavaliable for sale, selected pieces may be subject to a fair reserve price established by the owner. This condition of sale will be announced by the Auctioneer at the time the article is offered for sale.

Auctioneer's Note: Thank you for your attendance and patronage. We hope you enjoy today's auction and are able to make many advantageous purchases. If we can be of service to you or some acquaintance, we would appreciate your contacting us.

BEWARE OF THE SOUND OF SILENCE

From birth we are conditioned to listen for sounds. As children we are taught to "Stop, Look and LISTEN." It's not only sight, but also sound which may represent danger. Once we learn to speak, sound brings us information, pleasure, and signals of approaching danger. What we are not taught is that in silence there is also a message.

At an auction, what is NOT said may be MORE important than the spoken word. For example, during a gallery auction, a refrigerator is brought to the block. The auctioneer begins, "Ladies and gents, the next item is a G.E. refrigerator, 18 cu. ft., clean, and running. You've all had a chance to look it over. Looks good to me. Hula give me two hundred, to start em?"

Now the same auction gallery, but a different sale.

"Ladies and gents, the next item is a G.E. refrigerator, which is part of the consigned items from Mrs. Bradley. For those of you who do not know her, it's here due to her recent move into Senior Citizens Housing. Since those apartments come furnished with all new appliances, she has no need for it. She hasn't had a bit of trouble with it since it was purchased two years ago, and here's the original bill of purchase. We will guarantee it for seven days if transported properly (in an upright position). Looks good to me, now hula gimme two hundred, to start em?"

Now let's analyze what was said, and maybe more importantly, what was not said. In the first example all that was mentioned was its make, size, it operates, and it looks good. In essence, "You buy as is, where is, and as you believe it to be!" In the second example, you got the make, size, knowledge that it operates, the owner's name, reason for being there, seven day guarantee, and it looks good.

If you know Mrs. Bradley, you'll know how it was cared for, also the reason for it being there is valid, and that the bill of sale confirms it's two years old. The important sound or the lack of it in the first example is the SEVEN DAY GUARANTEE. That's a lot more than, "It's running and it looks good to me!"

It's part of human nature that we hate to blame ourselves. We constantly try to rationalize our way out of self criticisms. Excluding outright fraud on some auctioneer's part, if you're the type that constantly blames others for every mistake you make in life, it would be my advice to never go to an auction. It really wouldn't serve much of a purpose to add the auctioneer to your substantial "blame" list.

Listen to what's not said, as much as to what is said. In many cases more so to the language of silence, since that may carry the true message. If the only message this entire book accomplishes after the many times it has been mentioned let it be said again. It's your responsibility as the bidder and buyer to know what you want to buy, how much you want to pay, or if you need it at all. The auctioneer has to assume you've made those decisions, whatever they are, based upon some rationale he's not privy to or wants to be cognizant of. Its not his responsibility nor should it be. Its yours as the buyer. When you make a mistake, bear the responsibility, don't try to find a scapegoat in the auctioneer.

INSIGHT TO BIDDER PSYCHOLOGY

Since the science of psychology is in many areas still a nebulous study dealing with human behavior and much less exacting than mathematics, some of the discussion in this chapter will stretch from what is fact...to theory, and what each of us see's in their own world. Maybe it would be better stated, as each of us views the world.

It has been my experience and all things being equal, the items of an estate sold on the premises as opposed to being sold from an auction gallery, will bring 10 to 12 percent more in gross receipts. The reason is that the buyers that come to the on-site sale are in a totally different state of mind. First, they associate the items there with a individual person and more importantly it's the home location of the things being sold. Secondly, if they know the owners, the buyers can personally relate to the items sold. Thirdly, and more important than the other two, if it's a nice home, and well cared for, the buyers will transfer that into the condition and value of the items. Last but not least, if the location of the home is for example, near a lake or has a large lawn, the whole sale becomes a much more festive affair. These things all add to the success of the sale.

I had a auctioneer from Vermont tell me once about a sale he was conducting in the Village of Brandon.

"Hell, Frank, this is one of those tree lined streets with houses and people who look like they were part of the "Father Knows Best" TV series. I'd do the auction for nothing, it's gonna be a great sale!"

I'm sure the "for nothing" is an overstatement and not everyone can have such a setting, but the emphasis is on what people perceive and the mood it creates.

In the setting of the auction gallery, or barn, as some locations would be more accurately labeled, the whole affair takes on an entirely different hue. It seems as if the items lose their original identity. I suspect the main reason for that is the items are not in their natural or original location and are usually mixed with the belongings of others.

Even though my auction gallery had four thousand square feet of space, excluding bathrooms and the food concession, a fireplace, drapes, rugs, heat and air conditioning, it just never replaces the items natural setting. The mind-set of the buyer is that all the items gathered were there because they no longer had any use to the owners. It's a gathering, a mixture of things. Probably even God, nor the auctioneer know their many origins.

There have been times when I've done estate sales through the gallery, which could not be done on site, and were specifically advertised by family name. Some were comprised of all antiques, and they never did as well as they would have if they had been done at the home.

I find many buyers will come to an auction with a confrontational feeling toward the auctioneer. In their minds it's a competitive type concept as if he was the one they had to beat, be sharper than, and protect themselves from paying too much. In a honestly run auction...nothing is further from the truth. They have nothing to fear, because it will be they along with the other bidders who set the price. Heck, the numbers never end as long as the folks keep bidding and if it were your items you wouldn't want them to quit bidding either.

It always causes me some concern to see a situation develop where a buyer comes to an auction and because someone bids higher, a lasting dislike for that person is created. Certainly I can understand some disappointment by the back bidder of having to pay more, but not to the point of letting it become a lasting un-pleasant opinion of the other person.

During my years as a buyer, while supporting a family of three and trying to earn extra money for college, there were auctions where it was impossible for me to buy. I just couldn't. The prices were too high for resale through another auction. Sure, I was disappointed and certainly I needed to support my family, but none of these reasons were justification for a continuing dislike of anyone.

Yes, the auction system does create a type of competitive action between the bidders. That's what its all about. Unless someone has cheated or stacked the cards unfairly in his favor, it shouldn't turn out to be more than someone else seeing a greater value in the item. There should be no doubt that the auction game is a competitive one and one should be prepared for that environment. I've seen this type thing create friction between friends and relatives. Maybe in rare cases there is just cause to feel more than normal disappointment, but it would be my hope that these cases would be as rare as "hen's teeth".

After the auction, life and feelings toward others should be the same as before it. Who knows the next auction may result in the reverse roles in the same two people!

SHOULD YOU HAVE AN AUCTION

Yes! except if whoever is in control gave away all the significant items to the niece in Ohio, the daughter in Texas and the next door neighbor who mowed the lawn and now all that's left is the remainder from three yard sales, you may as well send the rest to Ohio, Texas or next door.

Above and beyond the reasons that it is the least expensive and quickest way to dispose of items. There are some other reasons for having an auction that deserve a closer look. Among the examples described in my own family and in others which will be discussed, are experiences one should learn from.

Rather than address those left behind, let the focus be directed toward those who cast that favorite relative or friend into the tempestuous sea like Jonah.

The thankless job of being selected to serve as an executor/executrix can be one of the most aggravating experiences of one's life. In most cases they fail, or those attorneys who advise the deceased before they become the past tense, drop the ball on the most important function, and that is exactly how the dispersal of the estate should be handled.

If I haven't made it clear up to this point, my opinion of lawyers isn't probably as great as it should be. In many instances in the rush to dot the legal "I's", cross the "T's" and collect their fee, they fail to provide any further guidance which could prevent significant grief later. One could be inclined to conclude that their purpose isn't to limit later legal discord, but create the possibility of it. Keeping this in mind, it would be wise to direct his attention accordingly.

I'm speaking here of the chattel property, such as the living room couch, lawn mower, stainless steel flatware, along with the antique roll top desk, and collection of colored Depression glass, and on from there. It would almost seem as if the deceased gives no consideration to those who remain as the living heirs and have to put up with the hassle brought into their continuing lives. In many cases it appears as if the deceased goes to great lengths to do the right thing and fails miserably.

By not considering an auction as a stipulation in their will, they inadvertently create a catalyst of disaster. The division of all the items can create havoc and hard feelings never to be resolved among the surviving family members. In addition those feelings of resentment of who took what or how much will tear apart the average family. If the division of the estate is left to some haphazard distribution, the dissension it creates is usually passed on to the next generation and then some.

Speaking now to those of us who are slated to go where all good souls who have adhered to "The Ten Commandants" go. A few simple steps can eliminate this potential problem by simply stating in a will that all furnishings and goods listed in a simple inventory are to be sold at auction. The proceeds are then to be divided according to the stipulations of the will. Since currency is the most common denominator, a dollar is the same as every other one, except its serial number, when divided among the heirs. Granted the monetary division may vary according to the will, but that's a private matter of the one who drafts it.

As an example, let's take an actual occurrence. Keep in mind this was a family that never bickered prior to the death of their mother. There were five children, four brothers and a sister, all married with families. The will was general in nature, stating that after all bills were paid, the proceeds from the sale of the real estate, a small bank account, and household furnishings, were to be divided among the five children equally.

It was within less than an hours of the mother's demise, that the executor was descended upon by those sharing in the estate, for various items including everything from glassware, silver-plated flatware, to small furniture items. They were permitted to take those things they requested by the executor, after all, how does one say "NO" to his brothers and sister. Some took one thing, others took more. The executor took nothing. Later, when the remaining items of little value had to be disposed of, the estate had to stand the additional expense of taking the rest to an auction gallery, since there no longer was enough to hold an on site auction.

Years later the executor admitted to me that should he ever find himself in the same position again, everything would be auctioned. In that way all heirs would have had the same fair opportunity to get what they wanted and the amount they desired. No one member could have been critical of the other over the amount that they bought. In addition, since the auction would have been held at the house, there wouldn't have been any further expense to those heirs who received less, to have items trucked to another location.

Since the proceeds were to be divided equally, the only cost to the heirs would have been the auctioneer's commission. In all probability they would have received equally a greater share. The inequality which took place of who took what and how much, stayed in that family and was passed on to the next generation. I know this to be true, because my father served as the executor of his parents estate.

In another situation, an elderly neighbor discussed with me the elaborate individual selection process she had devised to circumvent that very problem. The estate was to be divided among eight nieces and nephews. Each was called separately to select any item they wished.

Taking great pride in her project, she insisted in showing me the various labels, bearing the recipient's name. Giving her the respect earned by a person her age, I said nothing, but I knew her elaborate plan was doomed. During our tour, I couldn't help but wonder, who was called first, and who was called last to make their choice.

Whoever was last certainly would have had less to choose from.

If what I've heard through a small village grapevine is true, and also that those in heaven can look down on the living, then she knows she failed. She was barely in the grave when the parties descended upon her large home, not only to claim their items, but to see that others got only what they had coming. Some who paid their respects for the deceased and arrived late found some of their items "Gone With The Wind".

As I drove by I viewed the pick-up trucks scattered across the lawn as people scurried around carrying items, while the others stood watching. A rather offensive thought came to my mind and that was the only thing missing among the self-appointed security group was a video camera to record the event.

Two other thoughts filled my mind further down the road. "The first to be called had the greatest amount to choose from, while the last had less." The second thought was, "Was this what the deceased really wanted to create?"' Maybe she disliked them all, but knowing her, I doubt it. Her struggle to be fair was destined to fail and it did.

Another instance took place during the set-up of an auction I was doing. A twice removed cousin spied a First Communion Prayer Book of the deceased, and asked my permission to take it. I referred her to the executor, who politely explained everything would be auctioned so that all parties would have the same opportunity to have those things important to them. She explained how her life would not be complete without it, but realizing the executor meant what he had said, she left in a huff.

It was the executor's request that during the auction I sell that item separately, and to make sure she was aware it was being sold. My experience told me that this type person rarely wants the article if it must be paid for. Sure enough, during the auction, she sat in the third row, on the aisle. When the time came for the book to be sold I took great care explaining what it was, as I showed it to her and others. It sold for $3.50, and she never offered a single bid.

So why an auction! Because it's the fairest, and provides protection against creating the situations discussed in this chapter. Maybe there are those among us who really wish to create the lasting grief to the survivors, but I would rather think its just their lack of forethought.

It's the quickest, least expensive and best way. When

you get to the bottom line after selling everything, all the odds and ends, chipped china, nuts, bolts, and what have you the total proceeds will be greater than if it were done in some other way.

Most importantly it treats all parties equally and fairly. One brother or sister is no different than the other. Each niece or nephew share the same footing as the grandchildren when the bidding starts. No one is first or last.

"Those of my house are equal unto to me. I shall not make better one over the other, for they are all mine."

But if those of your house aren't equal, so be it. The dissatisfaction caused by the difference in dollars will dissipate much faster than that special item one received over the other. Unless there is some justification to punish some among the living, if not give them a choice of the dollars or purchasing what they truly value and let them arrive at that worth by their own individual judgment.

HOW TO CHOOSE AN AUCTION SERVICE

Much like many written suggestions advising how to win at poker, how to be successful in the stock market, or for a sure fire way to raise children, my hat is in the ring on selecting the right auctioneer. But the real point being, there are many claims to *expertise* in any field and one should analyze all which are available.

It might be wise, if time permits, to gather all the contact information about the various auction services near you. If you know anyone who has used or attended any auctions, get their input. Don't necessarily make a quick decision based upon that information alone. Apply the good common sense God gave you along with some of the tips in this chapter as you begin your selection.

It has been my observation that the most classy looking is not always the best. I found the same applies to horses, wives or husbands, not only auction services. An awful lot of iron pyrite has been passed off as gold over the years, not to forget that bridge in Brooklyn.

If the reader has not reached the station of maturity in life where he knows that there's nothing for nothing in this world, then I would recommend he read no further. It would be evident that the following information would do nothing to enhance their general knowledge about what makes the world turn. In this specific case, the auction world.

For those with a mature grip on life, there are two basic approaches. First is where the auction service has the seller pay all the expenses, and that can be quite a litany.

In this type of approach the auction service usually deducts those expenses from the proceeds of the sale. Some of them use a special kind of pen available only to them and some accountants. I think they get them from the guy in the bridge sales business.

Second is where the auction service pays all the costs from their commission. This is the only method to use. To do otherwise, might be putting the fox in the henhouse. The specifics of what might seem as a self-serving statement will follow shortly.

One must remember that an auctioneer's approach performing a hundred thousand dollar sale would be considerably different from doing one that grossed ten thousand. Buying in quantity or is this case selling, always produces a savings. Therefore commission rates would be different and so is the case where the auction service pays all the costs on a smaller sale. There will be certain proportional fixed costs that will vary little in either situation. Looking first at where the seller finances the sale. To the untrained eye, this may seem the least expensive way to go, but is it? This can be like sailing in uncharted waters with the final "Port Of Call" lined with hidden reefs and much less the safe harbor than you expected it to be!

In this approach the seller should ask for specific answers to the following questions. It may certainly take a day or two for the auction service to get the information. But,if you're told the answers can't be had, look for another auctioneer.

1. Commission fee for selling.
2. How many and what publications will be used for advertising?
3. Will they be in-column or display adds, displays attract more attention and cost more?
4. What will the exact cost of the adds be, and will you get receipts?

5. How many mailed flyers will be sent and what will it cost you?

6. Are you able to present names of people that you would like flyers sent to?

7. How much will the specific cost of set-up labor be? What will they do in regards to, washing china, crystal, small repairs, or waxing furniture? Or is that your job?

8. What will be the exact auction day labor cost and how many workers will be used on the day of the auction?

9. Do they supply a tent and its size? How many seats will be provided? What's the cost to you? Usually a bare minimum size tent would be 20' X 30'.

10. How many days after the sale will the settlement be made? Seven to ten days would be reasonable.

Remember if you request an immediate settlement you may get checks from distant strangers. In which case if any bounce, collection becomes your problem. Make the auctioneer responsible.

11. If there are items with a reserve price which do not sell, will you be charged a fee?

12. Will you receive an itemized listing of all items sold?

13. If portable toilets are necessary, who pays?

14. Will there be a food concession?

15. Will he provide boxes, wrapping paper, and cord or bailingtwine for buyers who need it.

16. Get in writing who's responsible for what.

If you give an auctioneer enough time to gather the above information, there shouldn't be any estimated amounts of your costs. If there is they shouldn't differ by more than twenty or thirty dollars after its all done, and that should so be stipulated.

Setting aside the auction, remember you're paying to put his personal business name before the public. When your paying all the costs, he may do all sorts of things to benefit his business.

Look at the second approach, where the auction service is responsible for all the expenses. Remember the cost of putting the auction on comes out of the auctioneer's commission. It should be evident that those questions regarding specific fees for advertising, flyers, and labor costs, could be eliminated since all of this would be paid by the auction service. However some questions verifying other things would certainly be justified and necessary.

Keep in mind the most significant aspect of this approach is that you have the auctioneer on the hook, to use common terminology. Yes, even under the first option the auctioneer will tell you since he's employed on a commission he hopes everything will sell for twice its value. That in itself is probably a valid statement, but since the seller is paying all the costs, he has nothing at risk. Think about it...you've paid all the expenses and in many cases he'll cry right along with you about the items that didn't do as well as you expected. Oh God! how he can sympathize with you in your moment of grief while justifying his feelings by saying, "I wish they would have done better, after all my commission would have been greater. I guess we both lost, but that's how it is sometimes."

In comparison, in the second option where he foot's the bill and in a sense he becomes a partner in your auction, believe me you'll see a different kind of professional performance. You have him on the proverbial hook since its his money that's putting your auction on. Sure, his fee may be a little higher, but then he's at risk, much like yourself.

By the time the auction takes place, with the advertising, labor, mailed flyers, tent and seating, minor repairs, waxing of furniture, plus other amenities, he will have $800 to $1000 dollars of his money invested in the *average small estate sale.* One doesn't need to be a mathematician dealing with nuclear calculations to figure out what the auctioneer must sell in total volume before he begins to make a profit beyond what he has invested in your items assuming his commission is somewhere between 20% to 30%.

In the first option, sure the auctioneer would like to see things sell well, but if they don't, it's no big problem. Sure he earns less but he doesn't risk losing anything or at least he's not working for nearly nothing. If what most would call; he broke even; he's still ahead cause his staff is paid, all the expenses have been paid while he basked in the spotlight, but most important, the seller paid to put his name in lights, so to speak, with the newspaper ad.

Certainly it can be expected that the auction service

that's investing their money will charge a higher commission rate. But, after one subtracts all the charges in the first option such as advertising, pre-auction and sale day labor, mailed flyers, cleaning plus item repair, tent and seating rental, and commission fee. The owners will usually find less in their pocket. Plus they will never get that extra performance had they selected the second approach.

PUT THE AUCTION SERVICE ON THE HOOK. Its the only way to go.

Many inexperienced auction observers might jump to the conclusion that the auctioneer with the largest crowd of people is the best. Nothing may be further from the truth. In theory all that's needed is two buyers who are equally interested in owning each item that's sold and have the necessary money. Worse is a large group that doesn't appreciate what's being sold nor have the money to buy.

All that glitters is not gold, so ask or make it a point to attend some auctions and evaluate things for yourself. Sometimes certain inferences can be drawn during the investigative process if you compare apple to apples not oranges. For example, one must compare the items of one auction with another fairly. If one is loaded with antique marble top furniture while another isn't, then hey. the auctioneer can't make a silk purse out of a sow's ear.

If a large number of antique dealers had nothing good to say about a particular auction service or never mentioned them in your investigation, maybe there's a message here. The reasons could be many, such as the dealers know they can't pool, thus keeping the price low with a particular auctioneer, or that the auctioneer feels a greater responsibility to the person who hired him than to the dealers. That gives some dealers a bruised ego, but to be fair one should give them their due. After-all, at most auctions they buy the most, but in most cases that's only because they take the time and effort to know the true value. The average buyer doesn't. Some auctioneers feel they have to cater to them while others think more about the seller.

Don't necessarily jump to conclusions nor consider what has been presented as the gospel. Things can be different in different places. It may be wise to read between the lines while doing your research for the right auction service.

There are some auction services who specialize in a particular category of item. If there is a large grouping of that item, or it happens to be the Hope Diamond it would be wise to contact such a specialty auction service. The knowledge as to where and how to contact those specific buyers can be important provided the grouping is significant enough.

Categories which might warrant this effort would be rare coins, historical memorabilia dating back to the Civil War, art, expensive jewelry, and early firearms to name a few. Information on where to contact such specialty auction services is available at the end of this book.

As an easy recognizable category, let's discuss real estate. This is one of those areas where special talent may be required. Those who specialize in this type of activity should be more knowledgeable and able to provide better service in properties such as industrial, commercial, bank repossessions and undeveloped raw land.

In a case where the residential property is going to be offered at the same time as its contents, that's the best time to do it and you don't necessarily need an auction service that specializes in real estate. There will always be a greater overall interest generated when all the items of the estate are sold.

This type of auction will combine two categories of

buyers, those for the contents and those for the property. Who knows who will buy what. It would not be the first time where a person who attended came for the riding lawnmower and the one who came for the property, reversed roles. While another who had no particular interest in anything bought the property. In cases such as these, most auctioneers along with the assistance of a registered realtor or attorney can handle the job. If he is a licensed real estate broker, then the auctioneer can handle the transfer of the property himself. If an outside party is needed the one hiring the auction service should ask who pays the cost of the real estate broker or attorney.

However, in cases involving unoccupied homes or vacant land, it would be best done by one who specializes in such auctions for the following reasons. First, they know how to present the property in its best light, through colored brochures and other specialized avenues of advertising over a wide geographic area. Second, for those which I have assisted, the approach of conducting the sale is completely different than the normal personal property auction. The auctions were held in a distant hotel complete with wine, cheese and videos. It's a collection of properties within a radius of one or two hundred miles with the sellers being banks, county tax departments, or private owners.

The presentations are expertly done with video taped walk-through's, aerial photography, survey maps and other pertinent information. This kind of presentation requires special expertise and is most important to buyers with various financial abilities and different real estate interests.

Since most property will carry a minimum or reserve price and won't be sold for less, this whole process carries an up-front seller's fee. That fee is not refundable if the property doesn't sell. If it does sell, there may or may not be some type of allowance regarding the up-front fee. This would be something to ask about.

The sale of real estate using the auction is no different than anything else. The appeal to those in attendance may include its desirable location, pure investment potential, or development possibilities. Yet, from behind some bush or rock may appear two persons who just can't live without the parcel. Whatever be the case, the bidders will set the price they're willing to pay.

There are both State and National Auctioneer Associations which can refer you to such specialists.

While in college, the head of the Philosophy Department dropped one of those pearls of wisdom that has remained with me throughout the years. It doesn't specifically have anything to do with auctions, but as the years rolled by I find it can be applied to many choices in life, including choosing auctioneers.

The professor, a man in his mid-sixties at the time, said to me, "Frank in all phases of life, man is quite specific in the selection process. In horticulture, by particular design a specific plant will be produced. In livestock, he will guide the breeding process to produce a particular breed. But, man's true folly comes in the selection of his own species. At that point Frank, he relies on a gut feeling called LOVE."

Although the analogy to an auction and love may not be completely correct, the auction world is not a place for "gut feelings," but rather for those with a more systematic approach. An approach based on knowledge of the items to be purchased or sold and the auction game itself. That's the only way to go.

It would be unwise for one in selecting an auctioneer where the auction service offers to purchase the entire lot, or those galleries which as part of their operation run a separate retail sales outlet. Most times this outlet or store is in the area of antiques or used furniture.

Some sellers would rather take the approach to sell outright. In their mind it's less risk and less hassle. Unless you're completely knowledgeable of the value of the entire lot and can negotiate a fair price, it would be foolish to enter into such a deal. How could you possibly know that Mrs. Garvey will pay twice what the cut glass is worth, or that Mr. Sorrel needs the junk lawnmower for parts. The auctioneer is more inclined to know, but if the auctioneer is made a silent partner as mentioned in the previous examples, he'll damn sure try to get Mrs. Garvey to do just that and Mr Sorrel to do the same. As far as the hassle to owner, it's all over in a matter of hours.

For those auctioneers who have their own outlet the auction business is a feeder for their store. Once the items are purchased by him or by another for him, then he becomes the dealer who wants to double his purchase price. Certainly doing that puts more money in his pocket rather than just working for his commission. Trying to cover both ends of the business, that of the auctioneer and that of the buyer, is like trying to serve two masters. Somebody is going to suffer and all bets are in favor that it won't be the half auctioneer/half dealer.

In the auction game he has a lot of wiggle room and

wiggle he will. All the squiggly motions will keep his sale outlet store stocked with some of the better items that come through his gallery. Many items will never be put up for auction. The consignor merely gets paid for the item at a price beneficial to the half-breed wheeler dealer. He can what is called "sell short". A couple of quick jack rabbit bids and "SOLD" to the person of his choice.

Take some time to do some research then give the auction service you've selected the time to do a quality job. The most common mistake made is that people think that the whole auction project can be virtually done in a week or so. To approach it with that as your goal is foolish. If you were undergoing heart surgery would you want it done in some hurry-up fashion? I somehow doubt that would be the case.

Ask for references and follow them up. If time is available go to one of the auctioneer's auctions. Keep in mind that slick colored brochures and other fancy presentations are not always the answer to your goal. If its just the matter of getting rid of what you see and think as a bunch of junk, then just do it and be satisfied. If your not completely sure, call an auctioneer. Even if they were fresh out of auction school and didn't know a hoosier cabinet from an outhouse you can bet your mother-in-laws skivvies two buyers will.

Making the selection of an auction service is not easy, but just use good common sense and consider the things mentioned in this chapter. If nothing else, hopefully it will lead you in the right direction.

AUCTION ANECDOTES TO LEARN FROM

This of all chapters was the most interesting to write, since it's actual auction life in the raw. These situations took place during my college days of buying and selling at auctions, along with the past sixteen years as a professional auctioneer.

There was a period of almost twenty years after receiving my degree that I never attended an auction. During the three years while attending college and averaging from four to five auctions a week as a buyer, I had all the auctions and auctioneers I needed.

One must remember during those early years as a buyer I didn't attend auctions for the entertainment, socializing or enjoyment. I was there as a pure businessman between college classes trying to support a family and somehow get a sheepskin.

As I reflect upon it now, it probably was one of the better times of my life, but either I wasn't mature enough to value it for what it was, or I was too concerned about paying the bills which come in early married life.

I've had the opportunity of knowing a few country auctioneers, that for the most part were an honest lot. I found them to be no more honest or dishonest than the factory worker that takes home some bolts or nuts, or the corner grocer who marks up the price of the frozen orange juice currently on his shelf because they had a freeze in Florida.

Some of these stories date back when auctioneers were accepting ten cent bids, and they made a living in an honest way. None were both auctioneer and buyer: they just sang for their supper. Between the dirt floor barns they used as galleries, the on-site sales, and hiring out as a paid canary for other sales, they carried forth a tradition from the distant past.

Most have since passed on, but those I knew didn't leave any rich widows. Yes, some may have been left with a collection of this or that. I have my sincere doubts that any were left with a Rembrandt or Monet.

These recollections have no special sequence, but it is my hope they will benefit both buyer or seller. They may only be unique in the sense that no one else ever experienced similar situations, or that anyone else would write about them.

The first that comes to mind is a recent one. It involved two reserve items I was selling in an estate auction. One was a signed Nippon cobalt blue tankard pitcher, which was decorated in 22K gold. The other item was a hand painted Bristol vase, also decorated in 22K gold. The daughter of the deceased had set the reserve of $225 on the Nippon tankard and $200 on the vase.

During the discussion I explained that the value placed on the Bristol vase was high for this part of the country, and that I thought $175 was more realistic. Since the total for both was $425.00, I asked if I was able to sell the Nippon tankard for more, then could I take less for the glass vase. She refused my request. The Nippon sold for $350 and the Bristol vase only reached $185, and she still owns it.

After the auction she came and complimented me on the conduct and outcome of the auction. She also apologized for her error in judgement, saying she should have taken my advice on the Nippon and Bristol vase. The total of $535 well exceeded the reserve of $425, and she had no sincere interest to remain the owner of the vase. I felt a deep sense of respect for her, since she was honest enough to admit her mistake.

Next concerns an absentee bid situation I'll never forget. At a gallery preview a woman traveled sixty miles to look at an oak hoosier cabinet to be sold the following day. It was in mint con-dition, and she wanted to know what I thought it would sell for. To keep from answering her question, I told her that at local antique shops they sold between $500 to $600 dollars.

After she discussed it with her lady friend while I busied myself with others, she finally filled out the Absentee Form for $375. Handing it to me, she asked if I thought it was enough. Had she not asked, I never would have commented, but I replied that I thought it would sell for more.

"Alright, I'll go to $400, but not a penny more, or my husband will kill me!" I explained about the plus one increment, but she refused.

It started at $275, going upward at $25 dollar increments. At $375 an antique dealer cut the bid in half, or increments of twelve-fifty, putting it at $387.50. The technique is discussed in an earlier chapter and used by some bidders to see if the bid will be raised again which would indicate that there were other powerful bidders. My next bid in her behalf brought it to $400 and her top limit. The dealer's following bid brought it to $412.50, and he became the new owner of the pristine hoosier cabinet.

When I called to tell her she was not the buyer, she asked what it sold for. I told her $12.50 more than she bid. I thought surely from her angered astonishment, she would somehow travel the phone lines and come through the handset. In an attempt to remind her about the husband and killing her, also the plus one increment, I never got beyond, "BUT!" The phone went dead, and I haven't seen her at another auction. Who knows, maybe another $12.50 would have bought it for her, but she'll never know. I guess the only thing both of us know for sure is that her husband didn't kill her.

During an auction of a boy's summer camp, formerly owned by the movie actor Buster Crabbe, of Tarzan fame, I came across a one drawer stand. Due to the dampness it was impossible to open the drawer. Also in one of the buildings I found what was easy to recognize as a former film library. It had been vandalized over the years, and there were no films to be found.

During the auction, I did my best to get a five dollar

start on the little one drawer stand with the stuck drawer. After coming down to a dollar without a taker, I jokingly chided the husband of a couple I knew to bid the dollar. When he did, the words "Sold To Number Six," shot from my mouth like a bullet from a gun.

The stand got taken home and placed in the heated garage, where it stayed for the winter. In the spring, the wife noticed the warped veneer and told her husband to take it to the landfill the following week. As he lifted the stand to load it in his pickup truck, it fell apart. Thus the stuck drawer revealed a film can with one of Buster Crabbe's movies.

Sometime later, noticing a new Oldsmobile in their drive, I stopped and was told the story. The little one drawer stand in part was responsible for the Olds. Probably not the lion's share, but it helped.

At an auction a dispute arose between two bidders, a man and a woman, over a diamond cocktail ring, upon the familiar "Sold" as it blurted from the auctioneer's mouth. My son, the auctioneer, made the decision to resell the ring between the two in dispute, explaining the reason under Rule #5 of the Bidder Cards they were holding. The rule states when a dispute arises the auctioneer has the sole discretion to determine the successful bidder or reopen the bidding between the two bidders in dispute. The woman's daughter became verbally abusive, even though it was explained to her to be the fairest solution to the problem.

The last bid of four hundred dollars was awarded to the woman, and the bidding between the two was started again. The gentleman bid $425 and the woman refused to bid further. After several calls, the ring was sold to the man for $425.

A couple days later the woman's husband expressed his displeasure over how the situation was handled. He also said his wife was prepared to pay up to $600. Although I attempted to explain legitimacy of the auctioneer's decision and beyond that the fairness to both parties, it fell on deaf ears. It seems that the only fairness some people recognize is their own brand, and that is without equal consideration to others.

Did someone say yard sale? Along with all the other things the auctioneer has to contend or compete against, now comes the "yard sale." Let me tell you a typical yard sale yarn, the significance coming not from the dollar value to be discussed, but from the fact of how frequently this occurs. Just as if you put your hand on a hot stove and got burned, if you try to sell and don't know what you're selling, you'll get burned.

It was common for me to do a lot of selling for pickers that visited all the yard sales for colored art glass at my gallery. It was easy for them since they could use the family car, and with an investment of twenty to thirty dollars, they would average about $140 to $160, after my commission.

One day I was brought four boxes. I told the gentleman it was going to be several weeks until my next auction at the gallery. It didn't matter to him, and since we had done a lot of business, he knew I would give it my best shot.

As I set up the auction and was unwrapping his items, a particular piece caught my eye. Looking at it more closely, I didn't know exactly what I had, but I did know it wasn't an ordinary piece of colored glass. I brought it home, and it wasn't until one-thirty in the morning that my research bore fruit.

It was my belief, after checking exact size and color, that what I had was a peach-blow bowl. I called the fellow the following morning to explain my feelings. Although I can keep my head above water in the glassware sector, it is not my strongest area of knowledge. I recall his telling me that he bought it at a yard sale for seventy-five cents. I suggested he withdraw it from the sale, and take it to an expert, possibly near the Boston area, one of the areas where it was produced.

A few months later he told me he did just that, and he is now the owner of a bowl valued at $1200 dollars. The moral of this occurrence is, if you truly believe the yard sale is the way to go, then at least hire an appraiser to tell you what you have to sell.

Here's a typical example of how one can save money buying at auctions. The ten year old Kenmore washer my wife had, just gave up one day. It just so happened we were doing a gallery auction which had a four year old Montgomery Ward washer to be sold. The elderly lady who consigned it to me was going into a nursing home and had no further use for it.

At the start of the bidding I notified the people I had an absentee bid on the washer. The bid was mine. I have a particular feeling about auctioneers buying openly at their own auctions. After giving those in the audience all the information I had on the washer, we began. Being unsuccessful in trying to start it at $100.00, I finally was the high bidder at $40.00.

My wife used the washer for four more years, and although it was still running well, I thought we should start looking for another washer. An on-site sale came up where the couple was moving to Arizona and other than some personal items they intended to take with them, they were selling everything else. One of the items was a year old G.E. washer. This time for me to be the top bidder took $200.00.

Having bought the G.E., I put the eight year Montgomery Ward washer in my next gallery sale. It sold for $115.00. That was three years ago and assuming the G.E. continues on for another seven years, anyone can see my equipment cost for washing clothes has been nil over the past fourteen years. That is of course excluding the other hidden costs of having a wife.

This example isn't a rare case, but rather a typical one. Yes, it's true that in each case if the washer quit working in a week or so I would have lost or had an additional repair bill, but I didn't think the risk in either case was enormous. Since in the first case an elderly woman owned it, normally it wouldn't be used much. In the second situation, the machine was just a year old. It would be unlikely for either to have been abused. In each case I knew nothing more about the washers than what I conveyed to the other buyers.

Another incident concerned a blinking eye clock cased in a signed Bradley-Hubbard cast iron statue. It was one item from a partial estate where the house had been designed by the former Frank Lloyd Wright. Trying to authenticate the clock, I referred it through a local dealer to someone he knew that specialized in clocks. By this time I had done some of my own research and had arrived at the conclusion that it was an original even though I had never seen one.

The dealer was quick to contact me saying it was not the real thing. When other dealers began to call me about the contents of the sale, I purposely did not mention any clocks. All of them except one eventually asked if there were any old clocks. Quickly realizing what was in the wind among the local dealers since he had to have heard about the clock from the other dealer, I told them I wasn't sure since the owner hadn't decided what would be sold. It was evident that a pool arrangement was developing, excluding the dealer who never asked about clocks. If anyone should have asked, it would have been him since he collected and repaired them.

Next I called Sotheby's Auction Gallery in New York

City and explained my dilemma. They referred me to their clock specialist. Once I explained what I thought was occurring among the local dealers, he was more than welcome to help. He requested photos taken from certain angles, measurements, and both photos and tracings of the signature.

Several days later I received in the mail a letter on his letterhead certifying the clock, plus a letter from Sotheby's verifying his credits.

Along with my regular mailed flyers, I targeted some out of state clock buyers who responded with Absentee Bids on the clock. Saying no more locally, the day of the auction came. In the back row stood five local dealers like hogs at the trough waiting to feed.

During the preview, the dealer mentioned before, who was the clock collector and I knew would never be part of a pool conspiracy, asked me what I thought the clock would sell for? I explained that my research led me to believe, taking into consideration how remote the area and limited collectors, it should fall in the range of $900 to $1250. He remarked that he was of the same opinion.

Stepping from the podium to allow my son to auction, I went to the floor explaining I would handle the absentee bids. At which time I described the clock to the crowd, saying nothing about the letter from Sotheby's.

My son, was still trying to get a $700 dollar bid, when the designated bidder of the dealers in the back shouted out $100. Quickly they chuckled among themselves as another $50 came from somewhere in the crowd.

The designated bidder of the dealers in the back took it another $50 so now we were at $200. Deciding that now was going to be pay back time, I raised the bid increment in behalf of the Absentee Bid I was holding and took it to $300. The pooling dealers realized now that they weren't going to buy it for a couple hundred. I figured they would want to stop around six hundred. I took them that far then cut the bid increment back to $50 dollars. They thought surely I was near the end of my bidding. Quickly I took them to $800 then increased the bid increment back to a hundred.

At that point it was going to take $900 to buy it since the $850 absentee bid I held in my hand was all played out or it would go to me in behalf of the absentee bidder for $800.

What I saw in the back of the room on the faces of the dealers pool was a sight to behold. On one was complete disgust, the other total surprise, and the third was blank. The designated bidder of the bunch was the only one smiling, only because it happened so fast he hadn't mentally caught up with where he was at in the bidding. The other three were reaching to usher him out of the room.

Lo and behold from right in front of me came a nine hundred dollar bid, it was the dealer who spoken to me earlier. He became the proud owner, and it sits on his mantle today. Out through the doorway, I could see the dealers' pool group having their money returned to them by the designated bidder.

Although most of my memories are fond ones, there is one that has altered what I will sell and when. In the days of the Cabbage Patch Doll craze, the long lines at the stores, the pushing and shoving between people and some reports of injury, were all part of that scene.

It wasn't long till someone got the idea to put one through my gallery auction. A $30 doll soared to over $200! Several others came through and they did the same. Everything seemed great until we did what we called a Christmas auction. The Cabbage Patch doll was the hottest thing in the country. It surpassed the hula-hoop by leaps and bounds. In fact as I think about it now, I never did learn to do that hoop-thing.

A dealer had bought a large quantity of new items, from toys, to hand tools, including all the necessary items to trim a tree, along with all types of colored glass items and wanted them auctioned. It was good for the gallery, since we had some box lot items which had to be cleaned up from some previous sales. I received a call from a local neighbor who had bought a doll not because she had any children, but for the monetary speculation. The doll was taken on consignment and advertised with the other items.

At the start of the sale I was surprised to see the number of young children with their parents at the sale. Much of the sale was going to be what we call "a hand out sale." This is a sale where you auction the first piece and when it sells for $12 dollars, and you tell the crowd you'll give them a break and sell the article for ten. Then you see all kinds of buyers wanting one or more in some cases.

It's a gimmick we use since the cost of the item was probably about three dollars. Sure it's a scam, but are we any worse than a jeweler that buys the engagement ring at $250.00 and sells it to the groom for $1075.00? To take it one step further, the ten dollars is usually cheaper than if you purchased it at the local retail store.

Back to the Cabbage Patch doll. It came to the block and my presentation speech should have taken some type of award. Suddenly it was over a hundred dollars and still going at $5.00 a pop. The bidding finally narrowed down to two people. One was an older couple who probably had a granddaughter in mind. The other was a young father of about twenty-five and holding a girl of five in his arms. A blond pony tail hung down the back of her frilly pink dress. Her big blue eyes showed the excitement and innocence that only children that age can display.

They were standing close by me at the podium. I never realized the tragic moment we were heading towards as I speedily called the numbers and scanned the faces in the crowd. At a hundred and seventy-five dollars, the young father quit....I saw in his eyes that "all done" look. The older couple bid the $180: I knew it was senseless to come back to him for another five dollars, but I did. He just turned and began to walk away.

As they passed in front of me I heard a mature five year old lady ask her father why they were leaving without the doll. He explained that he didn't have any more money.

She turned in his arms to look at the doll then turned away from the crowd and began to cry, holding back as much as she could, while asking,"But why daddy.....why?"

Thank God for sons who can auction. Stepping from the P.A. microphone, I went to the men's room as the tears swelled in my eyes. The incident still bothers me today, some ten years later. I hope I never have to experience it again.

From that day forward until the Cabbage Patch craze faded, we never took another Cabbage Patch doll on consignment. I guess it's a personal thing of being brought up during the depression and remembering a similar experience in my own life.

However, at an auction a few years later there were a few dolls in an estate we were doing. I happened to be in the rear of the tent taking a break, when a poorly dressed mother explained to her daughter that she couldn't bid more than six dollars on the doll. Another bidder took it to seven, and I jumped in at eight. The strangest look came to my son's face as he took my bid then asked for nine. Without any further bids, he said "sold to my father in the rear of the tent." When the runner brought me the doll his face also wore a look of confusion. I handed it to the young girl, her face beamed as she mumbled a "Thank you."

This next tale I've labeled "The Washer Exchange." During the pick-up of a small estate being transported to our gallery, the crew and I had to wait for some curtains to be washed before loading the automatic washer. While removing other items from the basement we watched the machine flawlessly go through its cycles.

When it came to the block, I guaranteed it to work, verifying that I had seen it work. It sold for over $200.00. The buyer was a woman I knew well for many years.

When I arrived home after the sale a message was waiting for me to call her. She told me the washer didn't work properly and wanted it picked up and her check returned based on my guarantee.

Needless to say I was shocked and first thought she was trying to operate it improperly. During the process of telling her about how to make it function, she interrupted me and said.

"I know how it operates. I have one exactly like it and the reason I purchased this one is that mine doesn't work."

After we picked it up and returned her check, I found it impossible to accept the fact that it didn't work. Having explained the situation to a friend who for twenty years was employed as an appliance serviceman for a national chain, he offered to look at it. A day later he called to explain the problem and assured me that it had existed for some time. We almost came to the parting of a friendship, when I was insistent that I saw the machine work just several days before.

Although a faint alarm sounded inside me and without saying anything to my friend, I took it to another repairman for a second opinion. When I was told the same thing, all kinds of alarms went off inside. From that point forward, when we sell such items we record the serial number plus put our mark in some inconspicuous place. Of course, the consignor was paid in full less my com-mission.

A doubly sad remembrance comes to mind. I was doing a benefit auction for a cancer victim without hospitalization coverage and without the normal governmental assistance programs. All the items had been donated by friends. It was the best grouping of items I've seen at such an auction. Articles ranged from Roseville, Noritake, to several pieces of Turn Of The Century oak and the usual used-nearly new items. Among the lot was a 54" round oak ball and claw foot dinning table in excellent condition. It sold for $100 dollars. My heart went out to not only the cancer victim, but to the contributor and as odd as it may seem, to the piece itself. Even though the auction was a huge success, somehow I still feel I let the woman, the contributor, and the table itself down, by not exacting a more fair price. It would have been a steal at $400.

In this business the worm turns quickly!

It was just a few months ago when an out of town heir contacted me about doing an auction. The site was a nondescript town who's notoriety seemed only important to those who patronized its convenience store/gas station. As I surveyed the site I kept saying to myself where is that main item or items that'll bring the buyers here so I can sell all this other stuff and pay for the day. The heir wanted the property sold also, which is always an "ify" thing due to the reserve and no charge if it doesn't sell. I took the sale just as a person going to the racetrack and betting on the long shot. As things progressed with the set-up I worried about just breaking even since I was paying all the costs.

One day out of the blue the heir called to remind me about a particular book among the many that were there, which at that point had not been touched. The following day I went to retrieve it. It was one of the local history including two other adjoining counties. It was filled with factual data dating back to the late 1700's and photos starting in 1880. After reading it I knew I'd found my key to get the buyers to the auction and once they were there I'd be able to sell them a lot of things they'd never think of owing otherwise.

The book which would have sold generally for $200 went to $750. That unusually high price set the tone for the rest of the sale. Even the property sold for $6000.00 more than the heir wanted.

And so revolves the world of auctions. As it turns, there will be humor, sad events, and others of a devious nature, but these are the things which make it what it is. Above finding them interesting, and fun to know, I hope in some way they are helpful in making the reader more knowledgeable.

THE HISTORY OF AUCTIONS

The invention of this incredible way to sell can be laid at the doorstep of the Greeks, so history tells us, around 500 A.D.

At least, whoever conceived the idea, certainly choose the right merchandise. Each spring a group of young virgin maidens were offered for marriage. Records tell us that if the buyer found out that she was not a virgin, after purchase, he could return her for a full refund. One can't help but wonder about the method of verification?

Next, the Romans picked up this new method of selling and refined it some with legal protocol. These refinements brought about certain procedures regulating the sales.

The English jumped on the bandwagon next, sometime prior to 1678, since that's when the word "AUCTION" first appears in the dictionaries. Of course the settlers coming to the New World brought the method with them. It worked well in the sale of bulk items such as lumber, furs, tobacco, and eventually, in the slave trade. The smell of human flesh and its agony being offered for sale under the auctioneers hammer will forever shadow the profession.

The coming of the Civil War brought more unfavorable light to be shed on the auction method. The practice of auctioning off captured horses, mules, and various other items was the method used. Now we find the expediency of the auction method used to dismantle an established social way of life. Quick and final ...after-all it wasn't property belonging to the North.

It became common for the commanding officer to conduct the sales. As other civilians took up the method of selling, they adopted the officer's hat and the title of "Colonel." The hat and the title established their place in history, as one who conducts auctions. Its tradition has become a trademark which is still in practice today.

Auctions have become as much a part of American life as the cowboy. Today they provide an entertaining, exciting, and somewhat romantic way of buying. The over-the-counter sale experience could never match its excitement or fun. Nor could it provide the tales to be told which makes each purchase different in its own right.

SUMMARY

I'm sure this book will foster discussion and debate as any controversial subject does. It will not surprise me that first eyebrows, then voices will be raised. I would consider it an accomplishment if from that for or against controversy, a better understanding of the auction process develops.

During the years of working my way through college, buying at one auction and selling at another, it became evident to me that many of those who attended auctions did so with a fear and lack of confidence to participate. There were others who did participate, but became confused and angry when things took place they didn't understand. That lack of understanding was robbing them of one of the great enjoyments of life. It was a loss to everyone, the seller, the auctioneer, and the themselves.

Much like that first kiss, your initial auction can be a pleasurable or less than so experience. The pleasure of the kiss depends upon many things such as toothpaste fragrance, the burger without onions, or general oral hygiene. Then there's that experience thing. The girl expects the boy to know, and all the while he's hoping to fake his way through it all and come away looking like a pro.

In a way the auction arena is the same. The setting is not the place to try and "fake it". Keep in mind it can be a unhappy learning situation, but it's not a teaching one. The person conducting the sale, even the honest ones, don't have the time to teach, they're there to sell for the seller. We all know no one is born experienced at anything and learning to become proficient is an arduous effort.

Remember in the learning process, the teacher comes first, then the comes the learning from the student. There is no questioning doubt in this case of the which comes first, "the chicken or the egg." This book is the time for teaching and for those who want to learn.

There are those who recognize that "Honest John" the auctioneer isn't so honest after-all, but don't know how to protect themselves from his slick and beguiling ways. All of these observations gave birth to the inspiration to write this book.

The buying process at auctions gives special meaning

and specific character to each purchase. It's the memory of bidding more for the antique table than the lady in the ridiculous purple hat. It's like playing Monopoly, and suddenly you're the winner. There are only two ways you become the winner, either by dumb luck or by studying the game and what's important to win.

An auctioneer's melodious chant mixed with timely humor, the frenzied bidding, and expectation of buying for less, all add a special fascinating charm, to be remembered again and again. It's like that first kiss, never to be forgotten.

It cannot go without notice of the countless estates or collections of items belonging to notable personalties which find their way to the auction block. The heirs of these famous people know this is the method which brings in the greatest return. Even those with unlimited imaginations couldn't conceive of an Elvis Presley yard sale.

Although the auctioneer is not a magician and he can't pull rabbits out of a hat, what he can do is offer a service for the dispersal of items in a quick and timely fashion. It's the method which will produce the most money at the least cost, while not leaving behind a mish-mash of items no one knows what to do with.

It would be reward enough, to know this book assisted someone in some small way. That some tiny kernel of knowledge was passed on which produced an enjoyable auction experience. To others, it will mean a more knowledgeable look behind the scenes. And then, there will be those who will repudiate its proclivity or premise, but let's all hope for the sake of the auction method of selling...they are few.

But, as a final effort I want to reach out to those of you that have never had the experience of buying at an auction. Believe me, this is where the true, total experience of making a purchase lies. When you're the "high bidder" and the canary singing his song bellows out "SOLD TO NUMBER 23" its got to reach down deep inside you and fill you with an exhilarating feeling you could never experience during a normal retail sale.

"Its mine! I got it!" That has to be the inner felt satisfaction of the buyer...but it doesn't end there.

Further on as friends visit your home and remark about the various items that grace it, you once again get that elated feeling when you relate to them the purchase experience. That emotional flush never ends nor its gratifying enjoyment of relating the story of how you became the owner. Its a thing to be held, cherished and deeply appreciated over the years.

I personally hope many of you enjoy those countless enjoyable feelings that many of my auctions buyers have experienced over the years. All of this has its value and in fairness give it a fair shake. When you buy a item from all the other bidders at an auction, relish the thought, that for years to come you'll be able to tell a story; a beginning legend of your personal footprints in the sands of time.

That legend will begin as so many I've heard. All of them have a little different twist, but for the main part, they all took place at an auction.

"My Grandmother, my Uncle or Aunt, my parents when they married were given this item. Now is your time to continue its history. Don't miss the opportunity, it will be a lifetime gratifying event.

ANTIQUE PUBLICATIONS

Listed below are some of the many publications that can be helpful in making the auction buyer more knowledgeable regarding antiques. Although the price information may be of some value, most significant should be the styles, identification marks, and crafting methods, etc. Remember at a given point in time, in a specific part of the country, during a particular auction----THE PRICE---will be set by the buyers.

Weekly/Monthly Trade Publications

Antique Week   Antique Trader
15 Catoctin Circle, S.E. P.O. Box 1050
Leesburgh, Va. 22075 Dubuque, Iowa, 52001

Newtown Bee
Newtown, Conn.

BOOKS (Available at most bookstores)

Schroeder's Antique Guide

Warman's

Grotz's Antique Guide

Knopf Collectors Guide to American Antiques

AUCTION SCHOOLS

Missouri School of Auctioneering, Kansas City, Missouri International School of Auctioneering, Dearfield, Mass.

Other Books

Shadow Of The Lonely--The smoldering latent passion in the reclamation of lost love creates a firestorm during the late 1800's western frontier.

When Justice Fails--Hired assassins by the U.S. government to stem the flow of drugs are betrayed by the same government who hired them. That betrayal extracts a high price by Frank Rodeen.

Justice Is Vengeance--No longer a government sanctioned assassin, Frank Rodeen is considered by some a threat to the political establishment and must be eliminated. Again those in government find the price beyond their means.

Contact
1st Books Library
205 North College Ave.
Bloomington, IN 47401
www.1stbooks.com
(800) 839-8640

BIBLIOGRAPHIES

1. The Auction Encyclopedia, Auction Research and Educational Press, Kansas City, MO. 1980
2. Wall Street Journal, 1991
3. Antique Weekly, PO Box 5001, Leesburg, PA 1989

ABOUT THE AUTHOR

Between the years 1957-60, in order to work my way through college and support a family, I became a buyer/seller at auctions. This is buying and selling was done exclusively through auctions, covering on the average of four to five auctions per week. During this period, I became intimately involved with the buying side of auctions, and to some extent knowledgeable about the selling side from the auctioneer's point of view.

After over twenty years as a Labor/Relations executive, I decided to take an early retirement. In my early 50's, I needed something to round out my life. It was natural for me to think of auctioneering due to my previous experience.

In 1981, I attended The Missouri School of Auctioneering, while my son went to The International School of Auctioneering. Upon the completion of the schools, we started an auction business.

Now after eighteen years as the auctioneer, I've seen the both side of the coin plus a lot of what's in the middle. The knowledge I've gained over both experiences, enables me to pass on to the auction buying public, the tricks of the trade. Those who buy and read the book, whether they are an experienced follower of auctions, or the beginner, will benefit.